Shackled Sisters

AISHA A ELAHI

This book is dedicated to all those women who don't have a voice. To all those women who silently struggle with their identities. To all those individuals who have loved and lost and all those shackled, waiting for a brighter day.

Thank you to all the brave women who granted me the privilege of your trust and allowing me in. I hope I have done your stories justice.

For Tracy: You made me the person I am today- I love you with all my heart.

My thanks to my wonderful Matthew for the endless discussions, passion and support. Jamie, your feedback kept me going. Nigel: for helping me in ways you will never know.

CONTENTS

Prologue

There will no doubt be those amongst you who will be shocked at the contents of this book and lament the day you read it. You may curse me for collating the stories; you may curse the individuals who wanted their stories shared, labelling them as fallen women. If those are your reactions then this book is not for you. Stop reading it. This book was written for all those other people who have waited, like me, for something like this to come along. A book, which tells you, honestly and openly, about the lives of Asian women here in the UK today.

I was always fortunate enough to have a large circle of friends from a diverse background. I started to see a connection in the lives of my Asian friends over a decade ago but like anyone else, I didn't think much of it. I thought, that's how things are, that's how that culture reacts, that's what is normal and what my friend wants from her life. To be clear, I use the term Asian to mean Sub Continental women (Pakistani, Indian, Bangladeshi), throughout the book and expand further on ethnicity and religion in each story. As I grew older and my circle widened, I started to see the injustices faced by many of my friends. I got involved. It wasn't much, just offering a bed when I could, lent money to women whose husbands controlled their every move, helping women to open their own bank accounts and allowing statements to be redirected to me, escorted some brave women (and 2 men!) to the police, advised women on where to get accommodation and support. I started to see how little people really knew about the existence of these women and how little understanding there was of their complex problems. I started to see how little support there was to help these women not just break free but remain free.

Occasionally, the press picks up on a forced marriage, an honour killing and we see the ugliness raise its head before quickly dying away again. The community pretends that there isn't a problem but there is. When you have university educated females, who have lived and breathed the same life a white female would living in the West, give up that way of living entirely to live a life with a man they barely know and become a submissive housewife- we know there is a problem! I watched in disbelief, unable to do anything, as blackmail, violence and emotional abuse were used to keep some of my dearest friends in place. They will never experience the life most of us take for granted. They will never experience what it is like, to be utterly loved by someone, or to be passionately kissed by someone, or to have the freedom to go on a girly holiday or to wear whatever they want, or to dance until dawn, to experiment with wild eye shadow colours and the latest fashionable clothes.

I wonder what you see when you pass a lady wearing a hijab in the street? Or when you see a plainly dressed Asian woman trying to manage a number of children as her husband strolls ahead. Some see these women as doormats, submissive and uneducated, others pity them, and some even fear them. These women are brave, strong, intelligent women who are trapped, through love of their families, through guilt, through blackmail, through fear of rejection, fear of being ostracised, fear of death and a fear of leaving behind everything they know to step into a western world that fears them. They are trapped through their fear of entering a culture which for most, is so far away, so removed from what they know and from what they have lived.

There are too many individuals living lives in secret, scared of the consequences they face if their western lifestyle was out in the open. There are too many individuals living a life under the constant threat of a revelation about their former lives. Maybe they had a partner before marriage, they went dancing, they drank alcohol- things most of us take as normal rites of passage. There are too many individuals who have no one to speak to openly, honestly and without being judged- we need to change this. We need to devise an outlet where these individuals can come together, free from fear, intimidation and judgement, and be able to share their stories.

Sub continental women, first, second and third generations, are in a huge struggle with their identities. This book is written for all those women struggling with their place and their identity in the world we live in today. It is for all those women who managed to live in moments of happiness, who managed to live in moments of complete freedom, who managed to live in moments where you felt alive before it was all taken away from you. One of the big reasons for writing this book is to let others facing similar situations know that they are not alone. It is to let them know that others have walked the same path as them and lived through the same hurts and the same pains

This book is for those people who want to make a difference to the lives of women. Read and understand their stories, their worries, their woes, their fears, their barriers and help them. If you work in a service that comes into contact with Asian women then understand the complexity of issues faced by women from minority communities for whom English is not a first language and who are uneducated. Develop innovative ways of educating people like Salma and

Ameera's parents, who don't understand the basics of nutrition. Help them understand this and we will see a drop in the rates of obesity, diabetes, heart disease and mental health disorders. Counsellors and mental health practitioners- when you see someone from a minority community finding the courage to come and talk to you- help them! Understand the many complexities they face as members of a culture that clashes with western values. Help them work through the guilt they might feel for leaving home, for having a boyfriend, help them regain their self worth and their self esteem.

Although I want practioners to pick up this book to understand more about females from the Asian community, I also want members of the Asian community to read this book. Those of you from the Asian community who read this book and want to make a difference, consider a career in mental health care! There is such a shortage of Asian counsellors, psychiatrists, psychologists and health care staff- qualify and put your bilingual skills to fantastic use! Teachers- for me, you hold the key to making the biggest change. Start when the children are young, tell them their worth and don't be afraid to challenge views. Recognise signs of identity crises and of suffering and step in. Be brave. Charities- there is some excellent work already being done out there but more collaborative work is needed. There is a dire need for a support network spanning the breadth of the UK that can be accessed by those in need. Work to put a support function in place to help those who leave their homes. Work with them so the guilt they feel, the loneliness, which comes with being ostracised, does not drive them back to an oppressive existence. Provide them with counselling, with education, with friendship, comfort and help them form a new foundation so they can build a new life for themselves.

It saddened me to do so but in order to protect the identities of everyone in this book, I have changed places, names and descriptions. The events however, remain true

1 NAFISA

Nafisa was the first born female in a family of 8 other female siblings. She was born to a young teenage Pakistani mum and grew up surrounded by the narrow, cobbled streets of Burnley. She is one my dearest and oldest friends, one whom I came into contact with almost accidently at the wedding of another friend. Her beautiful nature, generosity and kind heartedness made me stay in contact with her and she has over the decades, become a good friend of mine. She seamlessly integrated me into her and her family's existence, culture, troubles and happiness.

'The thing about Burnley was that everyone and anyone in the community knew your family business. The white people hated us, it's still the same today in general although the racism isn't as visible. The racist ones are too busy giving the poor Polish people grief now, they are the new targets I guess. We all just get lumped together in one big ball but people aren't as openly racist. A decade or two ago it was different and the racism was quite bad so you ended up sticking even harder to the Asians around you. You ended up sticking even closer to what you knew, to your own kind because the whites didn't want us. They didn't even want to live near us and would end up moving to a different part of town. Mixing with them- the *gorey,* was almost non-existent for us women but for men, it was a bit different. Dad became good friends with the local milkman and used to tell him stories about the cattle he had in Pakistan and how good he could milk them. Dad being the way he was would also tell him how cheap milk was in Pakistan, anything for a discount! But the milkman used to laugh at dad and say 'No no, your tricks won't work on me, it's still full price.' He was such a nice man. A really nice man. Sometimes, when we all sit together and talk about the times of the past I often talk about him. Some of my cousins, who are quite negative, always tell me that he was only nice to us all because we paid good money for bad milk. I don't think that's true though. I think he *was* a really nice man. The same cousins used to tell us that white people's skin stinks of dairy and mouldy milk. I believed that for a while and used to feel sorry for the *gorey* whenever I smelt cheese! There was this other nice *gora,* the insurance *gora* who used to come to our doorstep every week and collect cash from dad. I remember dad would give him £20 or something close to that and the *gora* would mark it in a little green book. Dad had about £2,000 saved in each of our names. It was probably the same as a savings account or something. It's crazy how things used to be, this man could have run off if he wanted but he didn't. He was a nice *gora* too. The elderly white people were mostly nicer to us than the rest of the white people.

I remember going shopping with mum and it was always the old white women who would smile at mum and smile at us, like a sympathetic smile you know? Like they felt sorry for us. It was the men who were horrible. I remember one incident in the supermarket with mum, she had to take all 8 of us with her because dad was out and of course, mum can't read English or speak it. Our job was to make sure the things we were picking up were suitable for vegetarians. We took the label 'suitable for vegetarians' to also mean suitable for Muslim's in general but had to also look out for the addition of alcohol and certain E numbers. We would all stop, in the middle of an aisle and begin a discussion on whether the item was suitable for vegetarians and whether any of the ingredients contained alcohol. It must have been a right sight- nine brown females, smelling heavily of curry, my younger sisters screaming, stood in the middle of a supermarket aisle with one us reading through the ingredients list…sodium, glucose, wheat, caramel colour... We would all listen attentively to the list being read out, ready to pounce on an ingredient which we knew or suspected to be *haram*, gelatine always got us springing into action. As soon as the word 'gelatine' was read out, the product was put back on the shelf. Well, I say put, I mean thrown back on the shelf as though it had offended us in some way. We would even shake our hands to get rid of whatever badness had been left on them from touching *haram* food. Sad really isn't it? It didn't help either that at mosque, we were often told of the new evils within E numbers and how they contained pig DNA or gelatine. The way we reacted to news like that was as though someone had stuffed raw pork into our mouths. I don't even know if any of what we were told was true and whether E numbers and childhood sweets did contain pig. Pork was such an issue that we didn't even say the word pig. We would say the letters P-I-G. And the biggest insult you could throw at your sister? You look like a P-I-G. Even when we wanted to offend, we didn't use the actual word. Really quite silly when I think back to all that.

Anyway, I remember all of us, standing in the middle of a supermarket, I was reading out the ingredients on the back of some thing or other and this fat, pink faced man came and pushed through the middle of us knocking me to the floor. I remember his words clearly even to this day 'Fuck off home you stinkin' Pakis.' Mum quickly got me to my feet and looked around for someone to come and help her –no one came. Everyone just carried on, some hurried past us. Mum couldn't speak English so what could she have said? She just put her arm out around the huddle that we all were, and pulled us closer to her. Mum's are really instinctive aren't they? I like to fantasize about that happening to me now, to my children. I would have plenty to say. I would not be the small girl

2

looking up at mum and this pink faced *gora,* feeling scared. I would give him what for. And tell him to go and take a flying jump. Mixing with the white people back in the 80's and 90's was rare. We are Muslims too you know so it's not like we can just go and start hanging around with them, going to the pub and drinking and stuff.'

Nafisa is beautiful. She has almond shaped eyes, porcelain skin and long thick black hair which falls about her petite shoulders. I have to always remind myself that she is the mother to 5 children, the eldest being 15.

'It's one of the good things about getting married so young I guess, as your children get older people start to think you and your daughter are sisters.'

Nafisa is 35 years of age at the time of writing. She was married in a small remote village in Northern Pakistan when she was 15. She lives with her husband and is trying for a 6ᵗʰ child in the hope of conceiving a boy.

'Personally I don't care what I have, a girl or a boy, but Shahid wants a boy for inheritance reasons and stuff like that. I don't know! Why are they so interested in just having boys? It pisses me off at times when I think about it so I try to not think about it all too much. My girls are gorgeous and I love them. They all keep telling me that it's the boys that will look after me in my old age but I don't think so. It will probably be my girls who take care of me. Look at me and my sisters! We sisters look after our mum whilst our brother pisses about smoking weed, chasing girls and getting my mum upset.'

Nafisa checks in on her mum on a daily basis. Her mum has had mental health problems for a number of years but no one wants to believe that this is the case including her mum. Having a mental illness within the Pakistani community is still a taboo subject. I ask her about this and how she copes with her mother.

'The thing is, I don't know how to explain to her what happens to the body when someone is depressed, how do I explain endorphin levels to her and how the random pains in her back, thighs, legs, chest and anywhere else could be related to her depression? I don't mean I don't have the courage to talk to her or anything like that, I literally don't have the words in Pakistani to tell her. What the fuck is endorphin in Pakistani? Or how do I tell her about the positive impact moderate exercise might have on her health? How do I explain the chemical reactions that will happen in her body if she exercises and how this might make her feel better? She doesn't understand the body, bodily functions or the basic things that happen in the body. It's so frustrating but then she was never educated so what can I expect from her? She has absolutely no idea what

3

a calorie is. She knows what fat is but sees it as the white stuff she removes from meat before she cooks it. She has no idea about how much fat you should eat per day. She has no idea about how calories, fats, carbohydrates, proteins and all that sort of stuff works in her body or what it does to the body. She has absolutely no idea. Can you imagine that? Not knowing that? If a person doesn't know the basics of the body or what a calorie is then what can you expect from that person? She eats small amounts of food and still feels hungry and so eats a little bit more. She has little understanding that the curry she cooks is made with *ghee* which is really fatty, it's basically butter. She doesn't see the oil in her cooking as being the same as the white stuff she trims away from meat before she cooks it, what can you expect from that? I can't expect anything from her, I get angry at myself for getting angry at her.'

There seems to be the same complaint from a number of my Asian friends. The subjects taught to Nafisa's parents within the rural, village schools concentrated on basic literacy and numeracy, the history of Pakistan, teachings of the Quran and recital of the Quran. There were no lessons on Biology and Chemistry, on Philosophy or Sociology, on Psychology or Gender Equality. Moreover, the subjects taught in village schools were determined by the knowledge the teacher had as opposed to a set curriculum. Individuals from these rural communities were lucky to continue in education past the age of 8- particularly girls.

'I do not have any memories of my parents helping me with my homework, or telling me about how the body works. One strong memory I do have though is when sitting in the park one day with the family and some cousins. I asked dad what made the flowers grow or more specifically, what made the daisies grow that we were making daisy chains from. His answer was to pick up a blade of green grass and hold it in front of my face for me to look at. He went onto say in his broken English 'This grass is eat by the cow, you see how big cow is? This little grass is food for the big big cow. What does cow do? Cow eat the grass and they make for us the milk. The grass make the cow have the nice meat, we eat the meat. When the cow have a shit'- he would always use the word shit, he thought that was the normal word for poo in the English language, he had no idea that it was crude or frowned upon! As kids, we used to smirk and giggle at him whenever he used the word and he had no idea! Anyway, so he would say, 'When the cow have a shit, the shit is the food for the grass. This help the grass grow and it go on like this', he would draw a circle in the air to symbolize the pattern. 'It is all God, *Allah ki Zaat*', which I think translates as Allah's creation. That didn't tell me how daisies grew or how grass grew, it told me everything grew because of God. I do believe it is all God's work, I honestly do, *but* I also get the science behind some of it, you know like photosynthesis

4

and that kind of stuff. Education for dad in Pakistan was learning about his country, reading, writing and speaking Urdu, History, basic Maths, basic English and learning to read the Quran. Mum's education was learning to recite certain paragraphs from the Quran only. She didn't learn how to read and write in her mother tongue or how to read the Quran and understand it.'

I always wonder when I speak to Nafisa about how different things would have been for her and her siblings if both her parents had a good level of education. I wonder about her mums deteriorating physical and mental health and whether this would be different. Nafisa had no particular interests in school and none of her siblings are in skill specific jobs. The hundreds of conversations I have had with sub continental Asian females have similar experiences relating to their parents education. Their careers have also followed similar patterns.

'Mum and dad can't speak English very well so we only talk in Pakistani when we all sit together. Even then though, we only talk about the things that affect us every day, like who we might have seen or what we have planned for the week, or what we are planning to cook on the weekend. Sometimes we get together and talk about things that are happening in the community. Or the upcoming wedding of someone we know which we have to attend. Or there might have been a phone call from Pakistan and we sit around discussing any news that has come from the village. We never talk about politics or some great philosopher. I don't think either of them would believe that there are such people as philosophers, and their job is to sit around and think.'

Nafisa laughs, a tired, wry laugh.

'Growing up, dad was too busy earning what he could by doing shift work and mum couldn't read so it was up to us to try and understand our homework. We couldn't ask mum or dad to help us because they had no idea. I remember in Primary school, I must have been about 10, I asked dad about fractions and he understood what I was trying to ask him but couldn't help me with the actual question. That is the way it was and still is today if I am being honest. I didn't go to college so when Aaliyah comes home from secondary school and asks me about Biology or Chemistry or Maths, I have no idea on most things. I tell her to Google it. Shahid got upset one night recently you know, he said our girls don't have a chance at making it big in this country. He was working for this *gora*, doing some odd bits around his house and started speaking to the kids that were there. Shahid was saying that these kids were so clever, he couldn't believe it. They knew more than him about world politics and history. He said that he saw the 4 year old boy of this man, use an iPad to go online, find

YouTube, type in the name of the video he wanted to watch and play it so it showed up on their television! Can you believe that? A 4 year old! My kids don't have a chance if they have to compete with that, even *I* don't know how to project my iPad to the TV! Shahid was upset, I think he saw that day just how different education is in this country for Asian kids. Its much better compared to Pakistan, but when you compare it to the education of the *gorey* kids, then our girls don't stand a chance. Shahid used to show off about his level of education before that day. He used to tell everyone about how he was educated to the 8th class in Pakistan, similar to college here. That is a big achievement for someone from a Pakistani village and in the community when people talk about Shahid they say, 'Wow, Shahid is so educated', but the types of education are so different. Shahid was taught about Pakistan, its history, the partition, Islam, reading the Quran, reciting the Quran and then some basic Maths and English. It still shocks me today that he has no idea what algebra is and no idea about things like Pi and trigonometry. I studied all that kind of stuff in high school at the ages of 13 and 14 yet he stayed in education until he was 18 but was never taught that sort of stuff. That's just one example though, there are lots of others like Geography- he has no idea how rain is formed, like the scientific process behind it. He knows nothing about female reproduction and how genes influence the baby. You know I have given birth to daughters only? Well, you know they blame me? They think there is a fault with me. My sister was going crazy at them all, drawing diagrams and trying to show them that the gender of a baby is determined by the sperm, all my eggs come out as X don't they? Depending on the sperm, the egg either becomes XX or XY. They didn't believe any of it though. My little sister makes me laugh, always crusading and trying to get them to understand or believe facts, nothing works though. Mum actually told her off for talking about reproduction and told her that women don't talk about things like that.'

Nafisa laughs. It always strikes me quite hard when I think about the disadvantage being faced by Nafisa's little girls. On the occasions we touch upon the subject, I push Nafisa and ask her to give her girls a little bit more freedom, let them go to parties when they are a bit older, let them wear skirts that show their calves, push the rules a little bit at a time. Let them know that it is ok to fancy the boys they see on TV...but she always resists my ideas. She tells me I am too modern and that the community is not ready for that. The men are not ready to see that. There are hundreds of thousands of Asian women and I suspect, a high number of men, born raised and educated in the UK who then go on and marry a relative from the Sub continent. The education level of these British Asians tends to be high school and possibly college. The luckier ones may well stay on at their local college and complete a higher level qualification and even a degree. Once they are married, the process to bring their spouses across to the UK begins. Children come along soon enough and the parents will pass whatever knowledge they have gained from their own education onto the children who grow up to repeat the cycle as their parents did. There is most definitely a shift taking place amongst the new generation of British Asians, who are more likely to obtain a higher level of education, who are more likely to work, who are more likely to marry later in life and marry of their choosing. Some things still remain unchanged though, things such as marrying a relative from abroad or where an individual marries of their own choosing, the chosen must be of the same culture, caste and religion. Having children is another must although having children in your twenties as opposed to having them in your teenage years is more accepted. There are still unwritten rules within the community, rules which dictate that a female cannot have a boyfriend, no sex before marriage, no drinking, no smoking and no eating of haram food to name a few. As a female you run the risk of not just being stigmatized, labelled and shunned as an outcast, but also being murdered in the name of honour.

Nafisa tried to break from some of these unwritten rules once. During our conversations spanning nearly 15 years, she has had moments where she talked about huge regrets in her life and about her past. But these moments were always fleeting. I have always been careful to not push her when she has not wanted to continue. Nafisa contacted me a few days ago once she learnt of my intentions of writing up our conversations. She said she wanted to talk about her past, that she felt ready to talk to me. And so here we were, sitting in the old coffee house with the surly woman on the counter who always seems aggrieved at having to serve customers.

'I am really happy with my life, I don't want anyone to think I am not. I am one of the lucky ones Aisha, look at my life. I drive a new Jaguar, we have just bought a 4 bedroomed house in a white area. I work part time and Shahid earns really well at the factory now. We have a huge 6 bedroomed house in Pakistan, sitting in four acres of land and Shahid gives me money every week to spend on the kids and the house. You know about Saima and them lot don't you? Their husbands beat them up all the time and go drinking in that pub in town- loads of people have seen the pair of them there. I feel so sorry for Saima and her sister, what a crap life they have, no wonder they are always smoking. It annoys me that people call the sisters slags, talk about them because they smoke but no one says shit to the drunken husbands. Still, she shouldn't have run away with an Indian, she was never going to get respect from her Indian husband especially after she had sex with him *before* he married her. You know he throws that at her all the time? *He* calls *her* a slag and tells her what a disgrace *she* is for hurting her parents! He tells her she is going to burn in hell for the anguish she put her parents through- can you believe that? She ran away with *him*! He didn't tell her not to run away with him, or to not have sex with him. He didn't say to her 'Oh no wait, don't do this, it will bring shame on your family', he encouraged it! Same with the sex, he didn't refuse it did he? He went ahead and had sex with her yet now, it's all her fault and she is the bad woman for giving into temptation and allowing him to lead her astray! I mean can you believe that? How the hell does that one work? Other people in the community say the same about her, they call her all kinds of things but why is it all her fault? Why doesn't he get some of the blame?'

Saima had been a good friend of Nafisa's. They grew up together and were both married at about the same time. Their friendship has faded into the occasional hello as the years have passed and their marriages were very different.

Saima married an Indian boy, her boyfriend with whom she ran away bringing great shame on her family. She was the talk of the town for months. Nafisa married her first cousin Shahid, her father's nephew, a few weeks after she sat her GCSEs at high school. She thought she was going on holiday to see her relatives and was quite excited by this prospect. She had last been to Pakistan when she was 8 and had enjoyed the experience.

'It's really weird to try and describe what it was like that first time we went as kids but, it felt like home. The earth was brown and red. People walked around without their shoes on and everyone in the village knew you and so looked out for you. We were like celebrities. Everyone from the village would come to see the children from 'London' - they thought the country was called London. We could go anywhere and the villagers looked out for us. We could walk into other people's houses and they would sit us down and talk to us about school and life in London. They would ask us questions like 'Does it snow there? I hear it's so cold that people die? Do you have a lot of money?' It was so safe. I spent some nights sleeping in the fields we owned. We grew sugar cane and some of the other village kids would light a fire and we would all sleep together, outside, in that field. It was amazing. Everyone looked like we did, spoke the same language and wore the same clothes. We ate the same foods and danced to the same music. We could just walk over to a group of other kids and start playing a game of some kind with them. I couldn't do that in England, the white kids wouldn't play with us. We spent the evenings lighting small fires in the fields and sitting around talking or chasing the animals or chewing on sugar cane. There were no toilets so we had to go to one of the fields and do our business there.'

Nafisa laughs and scrunches up her nose

'Pretty yuck when I think about how we live now but still, it was great. I felt alive you know? I felt like I belonged.'

We talk a little more about her first visit to Pakistan and the conversation eventually comes round to being back in England and starting high school. High school was scary not just for Nafisa but for her parents too.

'I was the first one, their first child going to High School where there would be white people and boys who would try and corrupt me! I think it definitely made it worse for mum and dad because I was a girl. I still have the photograph they took of me on my first day. The school uniform was navy blue and white. A navy blue blazer, a white shirt, a blue pleated skirt and tights. Of course, I wasn't allowed to wear tights because they were too clingy and showed the shape of my legs so mum had sewn some navy blue trousers for me, the same sort you would wear under a *kameez*. They looked like those balloon pants MC Hammer used to wear! Super loose and baggy so you couldn't see the outline of my legs. She had put elastic in the waist though thank god, and not a drawstring like the rest of my *shalwaars*. My pleated skirt was down to my ankles so where the wind did decide to expose my ankles or my lower legs, the trousers covered that right up! Mum had combed my hair adding about a litre of coconut oil to it. There was so much oil in my hair you could fry samosas in it! She pulled my hair into a tight, long plait which came to my lower back. I would have loved to have had my hair down like the girls do today but that was frowned upon and not the done thing unless you were at a wedding, in a Bollywood seduction scene or it was your wedding night. Mum would always say 'Good girls do not leave their hair down.' Mum and Dad were so proud of me, they were saying things like, 'Our big girl is going to big school', mum even cried!

Dad drove me and 8 other girls to school that day in his new minibus which was a good investment for him. The parents of each girl would pay dad £5 per week to pick and drop them off from the school gates. Dad was in huge demand within the Asian community. Other Asian parents, scared of what could happen to their girls, would hound dad to take their child too. Eventually, dad was doing three drop offs and pick-ups every day. We lived about 10 minutes from the school so no one was ever waiting for a lengthy period. There are times though where I can remember sitting in the laps of other girls in the minibus or sitting on whatever floor space was available. I loved school, I loved reading in the library, so much so that I became a librarian in my final years. I also started to like this boy and he liked me too.'

Travelling in groups like this still happens today within the Asian community-safety in numbers. It's also hard to play truant when you are surrounded by people who know you and your family and when you have someone waiting to pick you up and drop you off. To announce that you are going to be late home because you are attending a non-existent homework club is not a good excuse because the chances are, someone who travels with you and probably attends some of your classes will know there is no homework club, will understand that you are lying and soon give you up.

'I was quite scared of the white people at first and I was a bit disgusted with their tiny skirts and naked legs. You would see them, snogging their boyfriends during break and lunch times and I would be repulsed by it. Dad would literally have died if he ever saw me like that. I can remember my attitude changing though as the years went on. By the time I was in year 10, I didn't bat an eyelid if I saw an Asian girl and boy snogging somewhere never mind the white people! I smoked cigarettes around different corners and learnt to skive off during my lunch breaks. I also learnt to latch onto any after school clubs that were running so dad wouldn't wait for me and no one could say I was lying. I would only attend the clubs for half the time and then I would spend the rest of the time walking around the streets with my friends. The most fun came from walking home instead of being driven home. There was always a car, stuffed full of Asian guys, cruising the streets waiting for a bunch of giggling school girls they could whistle at or give their numbers to. I had so many of these idiots throw their mobile numbers at me. When I think about it now I cringe but back then, it was great! It was like receiving some accolade and we were quite competitive in our group too. I didn't pull this trick during winter because it got dark quicker but during the summer seasons, I was always at some homework club. I was good though, even though I was skiving and stuff, I would always get home at a decent time, get changed, go to mosque and then help mum at night to cook dinner and clear up. Still, I used to look forward to being able to walk home in the evenings.'

Nafisa met the love of her life during one of these evenings. He was out with his friends, crammed into the back of a tiny Nissan Micra. He would see Nafisa every day at school but never had the courage to ask her out until one summers evening.

'I remember it so clearly Aisha, I remember the wind was warm and there was pink blossom on the pavements and I felt lightheaded, like I could do anything I wanted. I undid my hair clip to let my hair down – I always felt like a seductress when my hair was down. I used to copy the heroines from the Bollywood films, who would hide behind their dark hair, and use it as a veil when they became shy or embarrassed. I always felt like I was breaking the rules when my hair was down.'

Nafisa becomes quiet for a few seconds.

'I still can't bring myself to say his name…. you're good at this psychology stuff, do you think that's because if I say his name I give him an identity and that makes him exist and so makes him real?'

I smile at Nafisa and say 'perhaps, I'm not sure.' Her brown eyes, flecked with pieces of gold, brim with tears and threaten to spill. She bites her top lip, opens her eyes a little wider before closing them entirely whilst taking a deep breath. We avoid the spill of tears.

'He was with 4 other guys in this tiny car and shouted my name when they all drove past us. It was a total rust bag of a car that sat too low. You could hear the bottom of the car scraping the road sometimes as they trundled along. They would always have some major Asian tune on, really loud, too loud for the car speakers which would hum, buzz and distort the voices on the track. He clambered out of the car and asked me if I would go out with him. I said yes. He then asked if I would meet him for a date at the local park and I agreed. That was it then, it started from there. All the secret Asian couples would meet at the local park. It was really big and there were lots of places where you could go and hide, sitting away from the view of the public. I think Asian couples still use that park in the same way we did all those years ago. He was so funny and warm and I loved the way he smelt, a mixture of fags, aftershave and mint. He taught me how to kiss. In the Indian films they never used to show mouth on mouth kissing and where they did, the actor and actress would just stand there with their lips touching. So when I first kissed him that's what I did. I just pressed my lips to his and stayed there for about ten seconds. He didn't say anything straight away to me but over the next few days, he taught me how to kiss properly. After he taught me successfully, he started to tease me about my 'kiss of death' as he called it. It became a joke between us, he would seek reassurances from me, as he was about to kiss me, that I wasn't going to give him the kiss of death again.'

Nafisa chuckles to herself staring at the floor. She then looks straight at me with a smile and continues.

'I loved the way his mouth tasted and the different textures of his skin. I loved running my hands through his hair and smelling his skin. He had this way of cradling my head into his chest and then covering the exposed half of my face with one of his hands and wrapping his other arm around me. I could hear both our heartbeats in those moments against the backdrop of the wind, the conversations of all the other students walking past us, the bell ringing, telling us it was time to go back to our lessons. He would kiss my fingers and my palms and my forehead and my neck and my eyes.

We would eat our sandwiches together and switch desserts all the time- he liked Victoria sponge cakes and I liked Flap jacks. He was always late for lunch so when he would eventually get to the canteen, there would only be flapjacks left. I would get to the canteen early and grab a Victoria sponge cake for him. He never learnt to get to the canteen early. The teachers would stride past and smile at us. I wonder if the teachers knew that our happiness was always temporary. I wonder if that's why they always smiled at us whenever they passed us. I don't know why I think that but they must have seen other Asian couples together at school and then seen them break up because of families, religion and culture. We were together for 16 months in total and they were 16 of the best months of my life. I loved him so much. He was so kind. Some of my friends didn't like him because his skin colour was quite dark and his family were from a low caste but I didn't care. He used to massage my head when I had headaches and he would cry with me when I was upset. He would wait outside my classes for me so we could walk to the next one together. He used to keep lots of different painkillers with him to help me with my period pains. I think I truly fell in love with him when he asked me straight out one day if I was on my period because I wasn't being very nice to him. I remember squealing with embarrassment saying he shouldn't ask me things like that, that it's a woman's problem and none of his concern. He said periods are not some problem, they are a blessing. 'It's how children are allowed to be born', that's what he said. 'It's how children are allowed to be born.' He said it was a natural normal thing and not something to be ashamed or embarrassed about. I never ever thought I would *ever* hear an Asian Muslim man talk about periods so openly. He asked me about my pains and I told him how bad they were. I told him how sometimes I would vomit because of the spasms so off he went to one of the Biology teachers and got a load of advice. After that, he would always keep painkillers with him and make me take them on time during my periods. He would give me some to take home over the weekend too. He was so thoughtful. Shahid has never asked me about my periods or bought me painkillers.'

Nafisa's eyes fill up again, quickly this time, and the tears spill down her face.

They rush quickly, down to her chin and drop into her lap. She wipes away at her face, still smiling, takes a sip of water and continues.

'He beat up other boys who said nasty things about me or about us and he would always hold my hand or have a protective arm around me during school. He was tough and had a large group of friends, all of them liked me and looked after me like I was their sister. He used to call me his Nafisa, 'You're my Nafisa' he would say, 'My beautiful Nafisa.' He gave me a gold chain he used to wear around his neck which I still have and when we couldn't be together, because we had a half term break or a school holiday, he would give me one of his t shirts covered in his aftershave. I think of him whenever I smell that aftershave. I still think of him. He eyes always had a twinkle to them and he had these little dimples appear whenever he smiled. I loved his laugh, it was almost a chuckle and would come deep from his stomach. Sometimes, when I was in a mood, he would sing songs to me. That used to always make me laugh, it never failed. We loved each other so much. I never knew how nice it is to be loved liked that until I was loved by him. You can do anything when you are loved like that. You *feel* like you can do anything you want to when you are loved like that. His love made everything better for me. If I was having a shit time it didn't matter because I knew I had him. And his warmth and his arms and his eyes and his heart. I could not see myself spending my life with anyone else.'

Nafisa stops talking and looks at me

'Ok this is the bit that makes me squirm but I want to tell you because I want it to be known. Asian women don't talk about stuff like this but I want to. I might not be able to look at you when I'm saying some of the stuff but I'll try.'

She starts to laugh with me

'I know, I know it's dumb, I don't know why I become so shy and stupid and embarrassed, maybe it's because I know I did wrong.'

I tell Nafisa to take her time and talk to me whenever she felt ready. This is not the first time an Asian female has felt uncomfortable talking about sex and intimacies. There is not a single piece of research on the sex lives of British Asian women. We do not read about their exploits in any novels or magazines. The advice available for this group is extremely limited and an area which is rarely, if ever, explored. A brave doctor in Pakistan recently published a booklet giving sexual advice and received death threats. Asian women very rarely talk openly and explicitly about sex and orgasms. Where you find a female who does talk about sex, she will refer to the act of sex as 'it', so they would do 'it'. Orgasm is replaced with 'one' so she might say she does 'it' and has 'one'.

'We did it at his friend's house one evening. I was completely ready to take this next step with him. He was so gentle. Everything he did, he did so gently. It did hurt, I won't lie to you, it did hurt and he didn't make me orgasm the first time we did it. Or the second time or the third time. He managed to make me orgasm though on our fourth time and it was really good. He had to really talk to me and tell me to lay back and not think of anything else except the sensations and to let go. I didn't even know what the hell he was trying to achieve. But I listened to him, trusted him and I managed to let go and it was just beautiful. I thought I had wet myself. My feet burned and the sensation travelled upwards between my legs. My heart was racing and I forgot where I was for a minute. I had never had an orgasm until that moment - I was 15 years of age. I always thought it was wrong to touch yourself and so had never masturbated. I didn't know my body was capable of making me feel so nice. My experience with him though changed all of that. I was masturbating most nights at home. I still, to this day, don't know who saw us leaving his friend's house. I think it was one of the women that used to go shopping with mum but I can't be sure.'

The Asian community is exceptionally well connected and it seems at times that everyone knows everyone. Within the Pakistani community this connectivity is almost an extension of village life from Pakistan. In a single village, an individual family will know every other family also residing there. The caste from which your family descends will dictate your power and influence in the village. The same caste title also acts as a family name tag. One of the more powerful and prestigious castes is the 'Rajah' caste, literally translating into 'Kings'. In India the same caste is known as the 'Rajput'. You could be a Rajah family living in a village in Karachi or a Rajah living in a village in Lucknow. A well known lower caste is the 'Mowchi' caste, with a literal translation of shoe maker. Like the Rajahs, you can find Mowchi's across the subcontinent. During the 1960's and 1970's, as sub-continental Asians continued to arrive in the UK to work, they tended to stick together based on their caste and their social standing. As the opportunities to work in the UK became less frequent, those from a higher caste were more likely to seize remaining opportunities purely because they were aware that those opportunities existed. They were more likely to understand what paperwork was required and were more likely to have the funds to pay their airfare. Their English and general level of education would have been better than those from a lower caste within their own countries. As an individual from a lower caste, you made your way to the UK either because you were helped by someone in a more powerful and knowledgeable position to you or as a manual labourer, thousands of whom were deliberately sought by the UK to fulfil the shortage in labour gaps left by WWII. The UK also pulled on medical staff from the Sub continent for the newly formed NHS. The individuals working within medicine in the Sub continent were highly likely to belong to one of the higher castes. Once you arrived and felt settled in the UK, you called over members of your family, all the same caste. You married someone who was the same caste as you and your children were expected to marry within the same caste continuing this cycle.

Nafisa is one of 8. Her father belongs to a high caste and was recruited by the UK in the 1950's to work on railway lines. Once he was settled, he called over members of his family - 1 sister and all of his 4 brothers who brought their same caste spouses with them. Nafisa's dad was able to secure manual labouring work for all of his brothers securing their passage to the UK. Nafisa's father married Nafisa's mother who is the same caste. Nafisa and her siblings all married individuals who were first cousins, children of aunts, uncles and other relatives that had been left behind in Pakistan- all the same caste. Nafisa's father was hailed a hero for helping some members of lower caste families gain employment in the UK as manual labourers, doing the jobs others did not want to do. Once an individual from a lower caste arrived, they became knowledgeable on the immigration laws and began the process of calling over their family members, arranging marriages and having children. These groups grew in size and although lived in close-knit communities, they were still segregated by their caste. Nafisa is able to tell me in great detail about the 3 streets, a mile or so away from her house, which are all owned by Mowchi's. She is also able to tell me the name of the streets where the majority of those living there are Rajahs. It is well known that members of the community justify the behaviour of a family based on their caste; 'They are Mowchi's, that's why they fight. They don't know how to talk' or 'Don't talk to her, she is a Kanjaree' (likened to prostitutes). Nafisa was often stopped when she was with friends and asked if she was the daughter of Rajah Yaseen of SultanPure. She was recognized via her caste first and then her father's name. A final confirmation would be the name of the village from which her father hailed. Her name was not required.

'It was a Wednesday at school and I had my GCSE's to sit over the next few weeks. I had already sent a message to dad via one of my minibus friends that I would be at a homework club that evening to revise for my upcoming exams. I was actually going to the house to spend some time with him. Ten minutes after the final bell rang, my name was spoken over the schools intercom system along with instruction for me to report to reception. Once I got to reception, I saw dad. He was stood by the exit doors looking really stern and serious. He said three words to me- no homework club- and I think I knew then that they had found out. *He* was watching me from behind a door with a small glass panel. I glanced at him but didn't look again because I could see dad was looking directly at me. The ride home was quiet. The others in the minibus were chattering as usual but it sounded really dull to me. It was a really numb feeling. I remember being able to hear my heartbeat in my ears. I think things went into slow motion for me on that day. It was such a strange sort of feeling. I was terrified. I didn't want to get off that clattering heap of junk. I didn't want the minibus to stop that day.

I went into the living room like I normally would and there was my mum, sat on the sofa surrounded by my sisters. She was sobbing, I mean *absolutely* sobbing. My sisters were crying with her too, hugging her and telling her to stop crying. Pleading with her to stop crying. Begging her to stop crying. Dad came in and sat next to mum. He took off his hat and held it in his hands, staring it at. He looked so old and worn out. I remember thinking how forlorn he looked. His bald patch on his head surrounded by thinning grey hair, the stoop of his shoulders, normally so broad and proud. He started to cry too. I hated seeing them like this, everyone so upset. I definitely knew at that point that they knew about us but I didn't know how much they knew. I carried on playing dumb and asked them what was wrong. My dad went first and said he had lost his respect in the community. He said that his reputation was lying in the gutter, that everyone was talking about me and that low caste black boy. I had been spotted by someone in the community leaving a house with him one evening when I was supposed to be at a homework club. I remember how hard my heart was beating and how my face felt like it was on fire. Mum went next and said things like, 'We have done everything for you, the school trips you wanted to go on, seeing your friends after school, we trusted you when you said you were at a homework club but you have betrayed us. You have betrayed us, your poor old dad, look at how hard he works to earn money for us and you do this to us. Look at him' she said, 'LOOK AT HIM', she screamed, 'Look how upset he is.' She went on and said things like I knew dad wasn't well so what was I trying to do? Was I trying to kill them? She kept saying 'I wish I was dead. I wish I had died instead of seeing this day, why didn't I die before seeing this day.' Dad was sobbing into his hands. I started to cry. I sat next to my dad and said 'I'm sorry, I'm sorry for lying but the boy was only a friend, he was helping me to revise. Nothing more, just helping me to revise.' I sat by dad's feet and sobbed there until he put a hand on my shoulder and asked me to swear by the holy Quran that I was telling the truth. I took the oath- what else could I do? Tell him I was having earth shattering orgasms? That he was the love of my life? That I wanted to marry him? And have his children? That I didn't give a shit he was dark skinned or that his family descended from shoe smiths? Mum kissed my forehead and said 'Don't worry, now that we know the truth we can handle this, just be careful in the future, our honour is everything and if we don't have honour then we have nothing.' I spent the rest of the evening in a daze with my head in mum's lap. She stroked my hair and everyone was laughing and smiling again. When dad returned from the mosque later in the evening, he sat next to me and held my hand. I traced the deep lines on his big hands and we laughed at some TV show together.

I sat the rest of my exams and became extremely careful about where and when we would see each other. We had both applied to the same college and we were both thinking of ingenious ways to try and see each other during the summer break - 6 weeks was too long to not see him. One evening at home, my sisters came rushing up to me and told me we were all going on a holiday to Pakistan for 2 weeks to see our relatives. I was so excited! Things at home had been really good over the past few weeks. I left in the mini bus and returned on time in the mini bus. I didn't attend any evening clubs, I just saw him during the day which was easier, because we were only attending school for our exams and had lots of free periods in between each test.

Even he wasn't concerned when I told him I was going on holiday. He said it might make the summer go quicker for us. We spoke for the first time that day about our relatives in Pakistan, who lived in which village and what their names were. His extended family lived about 200 miles away from our village in Pakistan. We only had one exam that day in school and it was first thing in the morning so, as soon as we had finished, we left the school and went for a long walk. Behind the school were lots of fields stretching out for what seemed like miles and no houses. We found a nice open field and lay down together. The sun was out that day and it was really hot. We kissed and cuddled and touched each other. I lay my head on his chest talking to him about our future and about college. We started to get excited about going to university together and talked about going to London or Bristol or somewhere far away. We spoke about our children, he wanted girls. He said boys were difficult and he wanted little replicas of me, little dolls he called them. He also said he prayed that the girls took after me and not him because I was pretty with fair skin and small features. I told him off for that and then started to kiss all of his skin, on his face, his neck, his hands, his chest- anywhere I could and kept saying that I loved him and his dark skin, that it was beautiful. I felt sorry for him that day. That was

17

the last time I saw him.'

Asking Nafisa to speak openly about her relationship including the intimate times was extremely challenging. She has never spoken to anyone, not even her friends about those moments. It is drilled into the individual from a very early age that this is not what girls talk about and that sex is dirty. Mothers do not speak to their daughters about sex. On the night of her wedding, the girl is teased and told by aunts and married females to expect some pain and some pleasure. Those Asian women who do have secret boyfriends and are sexually active are highly likely to either speak to friends outside of their faith and culture or keep everything to themselves. Countless anecdotal evidence leads me to believe that this is because of a fundamental lack of trust within the community. I am aware of numerous occasions where a female has been betrayed by their cousin, their best friend and even their sister when they have confided secrets involving boyfriends, sexuality and anything which could be seen to blemish someones honour. It seems that there are some lines that are never to be crossed. You are more likely to succeed in keeping your secrets between you and your chosen confidante, if your confidante is also indulging in the same things as you.

'My sister told me on the plane that the aim of the holiday was to get me married to my cousin, my 28 year old first cousin. She was giggling when she said it. She also told me that they had all picked out their material to have their dresses sewn for the big day. I didn't want to believe it. But I had a bad feeling that it might be true. We landed in the dry heat at Islamabad airport where some of our relatives were waiting for us. There were hugs and kisses and tears and more hugs and more kisses. We travelled for 4 hours to our village and to my mum and dads home. It was pretty impressive. Dad had sent thousands and thousands of pounds back to Pakistan over the years to have this huge house built. There were 9 bedrooms on 3 storeys and the house sat in about 20 acres of land. It was a white marble mansion equipped with fans, freezers, fridges, beds, built in wardrobes- all kinds of luxury things. It was ten times better than the shithole council house we lived in at home. When I stood on the top veranda and looked out across all the fields surrounding us, mum told me that we owned the land as far as the eye could see. I had no idea how wealthy we were in Pakistan. At home, getting dad to give me £5 for a school trip was a long drawn out affair. On my fifth day there, mum and dad both told me that I would be getting married to Shahid, my dad's sister's son, my dad's nephew. There was no discussion. It was stated as a matter of fact. I found the courage to say no, that I wouldn't do it, that I was in love with someone else and wanted to marry him. They seemed to already know this though and told me there was more chance of them killing themselves and killing me then allowing me to marry a black, low caste, shoe smith boy. I sobbed and I begged but no one listened. All of my family, my sisters, cousins and maids were all stood around me, listening to everything I was saying. But no one intervened. Shahid was working in Yemen and was due to arrive for the wedding in a few weeks. They tried everything they possibly could on me. Mum threatened to kill herself, dad had heart trouble and had to go to hospital because of me. My sisters begged me to stop making our parents so ill. They begged me to stop trying to kill our parents. I wasn't eating or sleeping, I just wandered around in a daze. All I could think about was him.

We had quite a few maids who did the cooking and cleaning for us, they would smile at me sympathetically. One, who used to comb my hair for me, would say nice things like 'Stop crying now beautiful child, this is the life of an *aurat*, a woman, stop crying now.' Another, who dressed me, would kiss the top of my head and shake her head. I saw her dab at her eyes with her veil so many times. I knew she was sad for me. But still, they never said a word to me about what was really happening. None of them ever acknowledged the reason why I was crying. They were all there when they heard me say I was in love with him but I guess, if they acknowledged it, mum and dad would fire them and say they were spreading lies about their virtuous daughter. I smashed one of the bangles on my wrist one night and used the glass shards to cut open my veins. All I could think about was him, his smell, his touch - him. Cutting my wrists didn't even hurt me. I felt completely numb and ok with what I was doing. There was no way of getting in touch with him. All my mail was checked and there were no phones, the nearest phone was in the town about 8 miles away and I was never allowed out alone, I was always escorted. I saw no other way out. I woke up in this horrible, dirty hospital with a drip attached to me. I had lost a lot of blood and felt really weak. My parents, my sisters, Shahid's family were all gathered around me. Everyone was crying. Mum was saying things like it was the right thing to do, I was the right age for marriage and that I shouldn't fight it, that marriage was a normal thing for a girl and I shouldn't be scared of it and do stupid things like this. Shahid's family, who had no idea what this was all really about, were nodding along with mum. Even if Shahid's family really knew what was happening they would never admit it or help me. After all, they wanted their son to start a new life in England. They wanted the best for their child, for their son, who had struggled out in Yemen for the past few years. I knew then that there was nothing I could do to stop this from happening. I was going to get married and that was it. My only other option was to run away in the night and hope that I find someone in the desolate surroundings, hope that no one recognizes who I am and takes me back and hope someone helps me. I remember thinking that even if I did make it back to England, I would lose my family. My dad, my mum, my sisters, my cousins, my friends- everybody. Shahid arrived in Pakistan about two weeks after I was released from hospital. I was eating a little bit more and even smiling at times. I had been there for over a month by this point. A month without him, my friends, my old life, my school uniform, flapjacks and Victoria sponge cakes. I think I started to forget him.'

Nafisa looks straight at me. I can see the contours of her lower cheeks move with each clench of her jaw.

'It does funny things to you, being in a strange country for so long. You have nothing but family around you and you are thrown into a very different sort of life. And the opulence! We had maids and everything was done for us. I had gifts given to me daily. My cousins and my maids would comb my hair, touch my skin, shower me with compliments, tell me how they wished they looked like me, how lucky I was to be getting married to Shahid who was a successful businessman. The maids would bathe me and always tell me things to make me smile or laugh. You become the centre of their world. It is such a different type of living. Forty two days of just you, your mind, the heat and nothing else....you *do* start to forget things. I found I forgot most of the good things about home. Instead, I remembered how cold England was and my cramped bed. I remembered how much I hated the rain during break and lunch times at school. I remember the tiredness of school and the cooking, cleaning and ironing of home. I remembered looking at all the nice cosmetics in the shopping centre and not being able to buy anything. This was like a long luxury holiday. I don't know why I stopped thinking about him. I went from thinking about him constantly to thinking about him occasionally. He was an ache in my chest, in my stomach. I would be free of him when I slept but within moments of waking, I would think of him and the ache would return. I mourned him. I mourned him like he had died. As the days went on I mourned less and less. I don't know why. Maybe I was somehow preparing myself to forget him. I don't know.'

Nafisa's eyes are not able to hold back the tears this time and I have to comfort her. Her breaths shorten and quicken with each quiet sob and the tears run down the fingers she is using to cover her face. She composes herself and apologises. She takes out a compact from her handbag and reapplies some concealer and blusher. She puts everything away and looks at me. Her eyes, shining, raw and red but her lips still smile that lovely smile. She says something about being overly emotional today.

'We had hired 5 tailors for about a week. They would sleep in the guest house at night but by day, they sat on the lower porch area with their machines and tools and would just sew outfits for us all. They designed and sewed all the different outfits we needed for all the ceremonies. We would have to sit with them whilst they measured us and understood what we wanted and then they would get to work. Asian weddings have so many ceremonies don't they? You *have* to have a different outfit for each one so those guys had their work cut out. I remember when Shahid arrived into Pakistan and into my parents' house. He came straight to me and said how beautiful I was. He gave me a 24 carat gold necklace and earring set as a gift. Shahid could speak English quite well too. From the moment he arrived, he took me out every day. He took me shopping and bought me nice things. He wrote me poems and sent me roses. He wrote me love letters and would play Indian songs from his car stereo, the lyrics of each song were directed at me. We would eat out every day together too. It was overwhelming. To have this grown man do so much for me. I started to soften towards him and a life with him. Shahid talked to me about Yemen and his job. He said he liked modern women and wanted me to have a job and my own money. He wanted us to holiday together in different countries and buy nice things. My cousins kept telling me how fortunate I was to have Shahid's love. They would tell me he was so kind, generous with his money and he would let me work too. Most Asian men are not like that, that's what they kept telling me.

I remember looking at Shahid's eyes and thinking how dark they were and not sparkly like his, he smelt different too. His hair wasn't curly, it was receding. He had a crooked nose and although he was tall and generally slim, he already had the start of a belly on him. I never liked Shahid's laugh. It was loud and long and shrill. I think Shahid wooed me for about 3 weeks. I didn't have time to think of him anymore. Shahid would take me out early morning and we would not return until late evening. I was always surrounded by laughter, gifts, joy and compliments. One really clear memory I have from those weeks was when my mum kissed and hugged me and said through tears that her girl was all grown up. It was the night before the first wedding ceremony. I cried the hardest I have ever cried in my life that night. I cried for my parents, I cried for him and the painkillers he carried around for me, I cried for the blossom on the road on the day he jumped out of that little car and asked me out. I cried for our kiss of death, for our lunches together, for his chuckle and the way the teachers smiled at us whenever they passed us. I cried for the way he never got to the canteen on time. I cried for the way he called me his Nafisa, his beautiful Nafisa. I cried for the plans we had made. I cried because I had lost him.

The ceremonies started and I was kitted out in expensive clothes and lots of heavy, gold jewellery. Shahid's family sent me many gifts. Clothes, makeup, household dishes, shoes, sweets – all kinds of things. No one said anything to me about the wedding night except an aunt. She asked me if there was anything I wanted to know. I wondered if she knew about me. I said no. Shahid tried to penetrate me that very night. I hated it. I tensed up and that just made everything worse. He got upset with me and said it's not seen as a good thing if we can't be man and wife on our wedding night. He tried time and time again that night and finally at around dawn, he managed to penetrate me. I bled because of how many times he pushed and pushed which worked out well in the end because bleeding is the sign of a virgin. His mum was pleased too when she came in the next day to inspect and wash the bedding. Shahid doesn't believe in contraception and it has never occurred to him that I might like him to use his mouth on me, to orally please me, to spend time on me like *he* did. Shahid has never made me orgasm. I stayed in Pakistan for 8 more weeks and returned to England pregnant.

I never saw him once I returned. Word got out whilst I was still in Pakistan that I was married, in love, happy and pregnant. I don't know how he must have felt or how he feels to this day. I heard from school friends that he had applied for and been accepted into a college in London. They also told me that my aunt had paid his family a visit within a few days of us leaving for Pakistan. They told me that my aunt humiliated his parents and said how insolent he was to dream of marrying me, of marrying into our family. His parents apologised to my aunt and fell to her feet. I cried when I heard that. It's not his or his families fault that his ancestors were shoe smiths. His parents were so lovely, so kind. I get upset thinking about it today. I still hate my aunt to this day but I have never told her the reason why. Dad was straight on the visa case. He used to put money into my account to show I had enough to look after Shahid when he arrived. He got his visa quickly, about 3 months I think. I miscarried my first pregnancy at 6 months. I was distraught and Shahid was too. We both cried. He has a good heart and he does look after me. I don't want you to think he doesn't. He *is* controlling with money and I don't like that he sends so much of *our* money back to his parents in Pakistan but it's not worth fighting with him about this. It was nice to go to Pakistan last year and see the house we have had built. It's around the corner from mum and dads house and on their land. We have 4 housekeepers there for the cooking, cleaning, washing and ironing. It really is a break when we go there. The girls love it there too.'

Nafisa went on to have 3 miscarriages over a 15 month period before she finally gave birth to her first daughter aged 18. She went onto have 4 more daughters at ages 20, 21, 22 and 24. In some of our earlier conversations, Nafisa has spoken about the stigma associated with only giving birth to girls. There were a lot of comments passed from other females within the community that were upsetting for her. Nothing particularly direct was said but comments like 'Don't be sad that it's another girl, try again' or 'Well you take after your mum don't you, she too had lots of girls.'

This preference of males over females tends to be because parents still see their sons as the main breadwinner and as the person that will take care of them in their old age. This care will come in the form of a daughter in law who is expected to live with her in laws and take over the household duties giving the mother in law a break. A daughter is seen as someone else's property because she will eventually be wed and leave the family home to live with their husbands family. This of course is reversed when you marry a male from the sub-continent. It is extremely rare for the male to not want to come to the UK and live with his wife's family.

'I don't want to try for another one after this pregnancy, if it's not a boy then so be it. This pregnancy is doing my head in, I feel sick all the time. Mum thinks it's a boy because my belly shape is different. She has also banned me from drinking coke in case the baby is born with dark skin! Can you believe that?'

Nafisa laughs in disbelief at her own words.

I have heard this from elderly women from the Asian community before. Drinking milk will result in the child having a fairer complexion but drinking cola will result in your child having darker skin. There has always been a pull towards being fairer. A fairer complexion is related to superiority, wealth and a high caste. After all, the high castes don't toil in the fields and burn in the sun. The racism present within the Asian community is astounding at times. Stereotypes are so entwined into the culture that it becomes hard to differentiate between ignorance and ruthless racism. There is suspicion of each different community, religion, sect and caste. The Pakistanis have a famous rivalry spanning back to the partition era with the Indians, however the Indian Muslims are tolerated more than the Indian Hindu's, Indian Christians and Indian Sikhs. The Indian Hindus don't trust the Muslims. The Pakistani Muslims don't trust the Bengali Muslims. The Bengalis don't trust the Indians. The Indian Muslims don't trust the Indian Hindu's and the Sikhs don't trust the Hindu's. It becomes more confusing when you throw in the differing sects amongst the Muslims too, the Sunni's and the Shia'ates, neither of whom trust each other and profoundly more complex when you throw in castes. I speak to Nafisa about this and her circle of friends.

'They eat pork though don't they? The Hindus and the Sikhs eat haram food and they all drink. Even some of the Bengalis who are Muslim drink and have boyfriends. I don't know. Everyone to their own I guess but I don't really want my kids being influenced by all of that. I have always said that my girls will marry whoever they want, within reason. I don't want them marrying some *gora*. They have to be Muslim but they can be Indian or Pakistani. I don't know about Bengalis though, I think I would have to see what the boy does. The Bengali's are quite dark skinned and around here, they are quite poor. I think Shahid might want the girls to marry one of his cousins, all of his brothers and sisters have children and most are boys but I have said to Shahid that we will take the girls to Pakistan and let them choose. I won't force any of my girls.'

I talk to Nafisa more about this and ask her if she really thinks that her girls will be ready for marriage at 16 or 17. I ask her what the chances are of one of her girls, who will never have been touched by a man before, saying no to a cousin who makes her the centre of his world? I ask her what are the chances of her girls saying no when it is likely that a cousin will be the first male ever to touch their skin, or whisper nice things to them, or write them poetry and shower them with attention and gifts, much like her own experience. She becomes very quiet.

'I know what you're thinking. You're thinking I am a bad mother for wanting my girls to be virgins when they marry. I *would* like them to be virgins! And yeah, I would prefer them to marry abroad! Have you seen the Asian boys around here? They are pathetic. I see them, cruising the streets, drinking, smoking, shagging the white girls. They treat women so badly. At least if my girls marry a cousin they are marrying into the family and I can make sure no one hurts them. If Aaliyah marries Shahid's sisters son, do you really think that boy will be able to treat Aaliyah badly? Shahid would kill him. And he would kill his own sister too. He loves his girls. I know I could be wrong about my girls, they might do what I did, I don't know. I hope they don't have to suffer that heartache. I made the right decision. If I had run away and married him where would I be now? His family couldn't provide for me. I wouldn't have any of the houses or the cars or the money we have now. I wouldn't have my family around me supporting me and looking after me. Honestly, I don't know how I could have coped without my mum, dad, sisters and cousins babysitting and helping me with the cooking and cleaning. This world is not built for girls, it's for men. They say that don't they, that it is a man's world? I need to make sure I do the best for my girls. If I had my time again I would never have done what I did. I caused my parents so much pain. I caused myself and him so much pain. Anyway, it's a chapter in my life that no one knows about and is now closed. Shahid will never find out, he would never let me live it down if he found out. I would forever be a slut in his eyes. I honestly think he would probably leave me.'

I ask Nafisa about this closed chapter in her life and whether she really, truly regretted him.

'I don't know. I'll never forget his smell, or his eyes, or his laugh…..I'm scared to think about it. It upsets me when I think about it. It still hurts me, even today.'

There is a long silence between us as she stares hard at the table.

'I think I will have my reward in the hereafter. Maybe he will be there waiting for me. Who knows? It wasn't meant to be in this lifetime for me, for us. I don't regret him though, how could I? I don't want my girls ever doing anything like that. It would be too hard for them. I get upset when I am hormonal but I hardly ever think about him anymore. I got lucky with Shahid. He loves me. I have a good life. I am one of the lucky ones.'

2 SALMA & AMEERA

The conversation below is between two sisters who have been friends of mine for nearly twenty years. They feel like old sisters to me now and I always enjoy their company as they bicker, tease, mock and laugh with each other. Both ladies are well educated holding Masters in science disciplines, both are unmarried, both have good careers and both live hundreds of miles away from their parents and their birth towns. Salma is the older of the two at 34 years of age and Ameera is 32, they are daughters of Indian Muslim parents who arrived in the UK during the 1960's to work in one of the many factories in the North West region of England.

Salma attended high school achieving good GCSE results and went onto college to study for her A-Levels. Following college, she settled in Oxfordshire and studied for her social work degree. She has worked since the age of 12 and continued to work evenings and weekends whilst remaining in education full time. Her earlier work as a new teenager was in a packing factory, extremely popular with the Asian community of Bradford. She worked gruelling night shifts, stood at a conveyor belt packing small varying items into cardboard boxes. The night shift rota was 10.00pm to 6.00am and the rate of pay was £2 per hour.

Salma: 'It was a really strange place. You don't think that at the time, you are just so pleased to get the job and earn something that you don't really take in what is happening around you. I had worked day shifts there but it was the night shift that everyone, including me, really wanted. The pay was better at £2.00 per hour so I was absolutely made up when I started the night shifts at 13 years old. There were easily 100-150 of us in that factory. Almost everyone working at the conveyor belts was Asian- Indian and Pakistani. Two of the supervisors were white and another 2 were also Asian. I am pretty certain that the supervisors were taking most of our pay, we never got payslips, it was just cash in hand. I remember reading the rota on the shift board that was in their office and seeing all these names that I didn't recognise- none of our names were on the shift board. I think that the supervisors were skimming from our hourly rate of pay, it isn't legal for a 13 year old to be working full time never mind working night shifts! Nowadays when people work night shifts, they can look at getting £10 + per hour so I think I was definitely robbed. Christ, I have been through a lot haven't I? Poor me huh? Does this mean I can also add exploited child labourer to my title now?'

Salma chuckles whilst looking at Ameera. Both sisters nod and laugh at each other.

Salma: 'Shit, I hope to God that *if* dad does read this book, he doesn't recognise this story as mine, I mean ours because if he does, he will be trying to claim some benefit for the abuse I suffered in this factory.'

Both sisters laugh at the remark

Salma: 'Dad is such a greedy bastard isn't he? All he ever sees is money money money.'

Ameera, the younger of the two has a quiet air of confidence. She is extremely intelligent gaining excellent results during her academic life. She went onto college and then University before completing her Masters in Computer Science. She has had some noteworthy jobs and is in a powerful position for one of the largest corporations in the world. Even as the younger of the two siblings, Ameera is the advisor and guide to whom Salma turns to, forcing honest self-reflection. The sisters are astonishingly beautiful in their own way. As I watched them saunter through the café we had agreed to meet in, I noticed how many heads turned in their direction. Both are tall, slim and extremely well dressed. Salma has piercing grey eyes, set amongst dark, thick lashes. She is wearing some of the largest earrings I have ever seen. The 6 inches of gold droplets covered with amethyst and crystal stones mingle with her curls, flashing at you whenever she moves her head. Salma has extremely pale skin and a smattering of light brown freckles on her body, features which drew admiration from her family and the wider community when she was younger. She wears a beautiful long skirt of purple, turquoise, green and gold with a chiffon cream t-shirt exposing the thin strapped white camisole beneath. It is hard to believe she is past 25 years of age.

Ameera is dressed in jeans, a smart blazer and low black heels. She wears small diamond earrings and her hair is loosely secured in a low bun. She has intelligent hazel eyes and a beautiful smile. She has a very elegant, old school beauty and is so graceful. I comment on how attractive they both still look and how I always think that whenever I see them. I ask them whether they find their looks difficult to deal with.

Salma: 'You do don't you Ameera? I think Ameera does more than me. I'm just so used it now, it pisses me off when some men just stare, the Asians are by far the worst. The Asian men, they gawp at you, shout at you, just come up to you and give their number or shout Oi at you, not even a conversation or anything. It is so cocky and so unattractive.'

Ameera: 'Yeah, I would be lying if I said it didn't faze me but it does cause me some bother. I really don't like people looking at me. Well, looking is ok I suppose, it's the staring that really unnerves me. Men and women both do it. I just try to keep my head down and not make eye contact. The Asian blokes don't bother me too much anymore though. I'm pretty sure it's because they think I'm not Asian. Neither of us look as though we might have some Indian blood in us now. It's interesting because I remember getting hit on all the time when I was at school and college but during and after University, the Asian men stopped. I think it's because we are too modern for the majority of Asian men out there. We were compatible when we had a high school and college education and in their league but after that, we were out of their league. Or maybe it was because we were too old at 18. Who knows eh? In my work circle now I rarely see Asian men and where I do, they are seeing a white girl. For me now, whenever I drive home to see mum and dad and pass the countless number of Asian men sat in cars or walking around, I think of them as belonging in a different world, not my world. Salma's quite funny though, I've witnessed her once shouting obscenities at this guy who was staring at us and grinning. I told her off! She came across as an angry, crazy woman!! Shouting at this Indian man who just carried on grinning at her and making kissing faces- yuck.'

Salma: 'I totally agree with you, I haven't met a single Asian bloke that I would consider having a relationship with. Or that I could have a future with where we would both be happy with our roles. There are a fair few of them in Coventry but so many are uneducated and still hold their stupid, out-dated beliefs about where a woman's place should be. The cultural beliefs are the ones that really fuck me off. I've met really successful Asian businessmen who are modern, educated but still think an Asian girl shouldn't have boyfriends or pre marital sex or a strong career. Working part time in a shop is ok by them but not a proper career. And they expect you to live with them and *their* families after marriage so you can cook and clean for him and his family. Even mum and dad say that don't they Ameera? We get the same whining and whinging from them; what are you doing with your lives, you two are so old now, I can't face the community, why are you working so much, why won't you get married, why are you trying to send me to my grave blah blah blah- the fucking wankers.'

Salma looks angry and apologises to me. Ameera is watching her sister intently. Salma excuses herself from our table to have a cigarette outside.

Ameera: 'Can you guess what's really going on? They are pressurising her to get married again, it is such a sore point. She keeps telling them she just isn't ready but that's not good enough for mum and dad. Mum cries a lot whenever we visit home. She even said that according to Islam, her and dad are going to burn in hell because by refusing to get married, we are not allowing them to fulfil their responsibilities as parents. That's not Islam! She's confusing her religion with her culture yet again. Her culture is crazy in parts and full of old wives tales. You know that Salma is a practising Muslim so when mum says stuff like that I think it impacts her quite a lot. I try to limit my visits to mum and dad to once every few months. The burning in hell shit is laughable. When Salma said she just isn't ready to settle down yet, they bargained with her and said 'Well, why don't you just come to India and marry one of your cousins? Get them into the country and if it isn't right for you then after he gets his British citizenship, you can divorce him' - pathetic huh? Trading their daughters like they are commodities.'

She pauses for a few seconds staring at her coffee.

Ameera: 'Actually that isn't completely fair. I feel sorry for my parents, the pressure they are under from their families in India must be unbearable. The poverty in India is something which we will never be able to truly comprehend because we have such a markedly better quality of life here. I always think of what I would do if I was born into that sort of absolute poverty with my sister. If I was fortunate enough to marry and start a life in a country like England whilst my sister, nieces and nephews had to face the daily grind of poverty and no hope then what would I do? My heart would break for my sister and I would probably try and get her or one of her children here, give them a fighting chance…would I behave towards my children in the same way my parents behave towards us? I don't know. If I wasn't educated then perhaps I would. If the culture was more deeply engrained in me then yes, perhaps. I don't know. It must be hard for them, mum and dad didn't have the freedom we have or the lifestyle or the education. Their lives have revolved around religion, culture and looking after family. There is a lot of sacrifice, personal sacrifices that are made. Mum reminds us of how she has had to do things she didn't want to do but they were the right things to do such as staying with dad even when he was kicking the shit out of her. She tells me that this life is not about doing what we want to, it is about doing what we *have* to do. Like marrying a first cousin.'

Salma returns smelling of cigarettes, flowery perfume and peppermint chewing gum.

Salma: 'I don't want to talk about the whole marriage bullshit, that's for another day. I did remember something though, going back to talking about the pervy Asian men. Ameera, do you remember that day when we were walking back from the market on Saturday and had to walk through Nat Lane? And that *freshy* was stood at his door with his hand down his *shalwaar*. Ha ha do you remember what he said?'

Ameera: 'Oh god, I do! Ha ha, he said 'Hai hai chicken fry' didn't he? With that head of his nodding away and a huge grin showing us his dirty teeth- he even winked!'

Both sisters laugh hysterically

Salma: 'What a freak! Do you remember how mum laughed and slapped her forehead when we told her? She was swearing away wasn't she? Called him and his ancestors every name she could think of.'

Ameera tells me that quite often, absurd things would be said to them which would make little sense if you were not from the culture. 'Chicken fry' was a lyric from a song that was popular then. A Bollywood director had managed to sign Samantha Fox, the glamour girl, for a movie and she had a infamous hit song which went something along the lines of, 'You are my chicken fry, you are my fish fry, I am never going to say bye bye bye.' They tell me this was probably the start of Bollywood attempting to portray itself as modern and western by adding random English lyrics to their songs. Popular in India with the Indians, the song came across to these shores but never had the same impact as it did in India. It had more of a comical appeal here. So when this 'freshy'- a term for someone fresh off the boat, saw the girls, he attempted to flirt by saying hai hai chicken fry. They have also been called juicy samosas and very minty chutney.

The sisters decide to talk about their early childhood and growing up in England in the late 1980's and the 1990's.

Salma: 'Do you remember the house on Stewart St? Fuckin' shithole.'

Both laugh and agree with the descriptive.

Ameera: 'It was damp and cold and we had a guest rat- it was massive. The little shit would pop out whenever mum had all manner of artery clogging, fried food out for her friends who were visiting. Mum's friends would just shriek and jump on top of the sofas.'

Both sisters are now nodding and laughing

Salma: 'That fat friend of mums, Shamsa, she was a greedy get wasn't she? She would turn up every week and eat a shit load of samosas. I remember she nearly broke the sofa when she tried to stand on it away from the rat. She carried on shrieking and then momentarily stopping to eat her samosa-the fatty! She used to turn her nose up at everything we had. She used to say she couldn't see the TV because it was too small, hers was a cinema or some bullshit. I remember her laughing at our phone too because it wasn't cordless.'

Ameera: 'Was that the white phone dad got from auction for 10p?'

Salma: 'Yup.'

They both laugh again

Salma: 'He was always buying some junk from the auctions. He brought home games that didn't work, a massive camera that was broken and once, a bag full of different coloured door handles- all manner of crap. Hey you remember mosque?'

Attending mosque is common for Muslim children. Mosque classes take place during the evenings and although the frequency of classes varies from area to area, most run every evening Monday to Friday 5.30-7.30pm. There are some areas where the density of the Asian community is greater and in these areas, mosque can start at 5.00pm and finish at 8.00pm. Mosque for Salma and Ameera was 5.00pm-7.30pm, five nights a week. The sexes are kept segregated (depending again on the area and the capacity of each mosque), and children are taught the Quran, teachings of the prophet and the Islamic way by which to live your life.

Ameera: 'I hated mosque. I never understood the purpose of it. When I think back to what it was like….. I think things are much better now for the children but for us, it was horrible. School was tough and you would get home in time for some food and then it was time to put the *burka* on, pick up the mosque books and walk to mosque. We used to walk there together. We were both in the same class with about 30 other girls and had to recite paragraphs from the Quran. Homework used to be to read a particular paragraph from the Quran and get the recital right. Pronunciation and everything like that had to be right. To this day, I don't understand what I am reciting. The Quran is written in Arabic so we had to learn how to read the words and how to correctly pronounce them but we never learnt the meanings of the words. It was like chanting things without having any understanding of what we were chanting. You can give me a book in Arabic today and I will read what is in the book but won't be able to tell you what the book is about. Of course, in places where Arabic is the main language, people will understand the Quran but not for people like us. A minority community living in an English speaking, Christian country. I think the majority of the teachers in the mosque, the *Maulvi's*, couldn't interpret Arabic either. They could recite it perfectly but couldn't tell you what a particular sentence meant. The Quran is pretty much like the Bible, full of stories which the *Maulvi's* would tell us about but in a 'It's now story time' kind of way and not a direct sentence to sentence translation.'

Salma: 'As I became older and after I finished mosque, I bought myself an English version of the Quran. They must have been quite rare to get hold of when we were at mosque. The translation is decent but you can still interpret it a hundred and one ways like any of the holy books. Ameera, I don't know why you're saying you didn't learn anything, you must have done. Remember those sayings like purity is half of faith? If anything, I think the Quran and Islam teach individual's to be good, to do good things and be kind to people, respect your parents etc. I know there are rules like don't take drugs and drink alcohol but that is more for your health. That's one of the things that make me angry when I read the press or talk to people who think I blindly choose not to drink because my religion commands it. My religion *does* say not to drink alcohol but it also explains that the reason for this is the intoxication that occurs and how this can make you lose your inhibitions and do things you might regret. I would rather be in control of myself and my actions. I don't think I ever thought, 'I don't like mosque', I think it was just something that we had to do and had no choice over. It was and I guess still is, the normal thing to do for a Muslim child. You go to school, come home, eat and then go to mosque, finish mosque, go home, eat some fruit or something and then bed. I didn't like the beatings but again, it was normal and part of mosque. If you didn't learn your homework, you got hit with a stick or a pipe, do you remember those?'

Ameera: 'God yeah! I remember the thin wooden stick one of the *maulvi's* had and can remember clearly, he had nailed 4 or 5 short nails into the end so the pointy parts protruded out of the bottom. He would make us put our hands out to him, palm upwards, so he could hit our hands with them. The nails would make my hands bleed. The pipe was just that- a grey coloured cylindrical pipe, about a metre in length and 4 or 5 inches in diameter. That would sting like hell. I remember the *patlas* too, wooden benches about 3 feet high placed in the rooms in a square fashion. We sat on the floor behind the *patlas* and would put our Qurans, books etc on them. Sitting on the floor was annoying, I'd always get pins and needles. The burka would annoy me too, my hair would show right at the top or stick out from the sides and I would get a smack for that. You wet yourself once didn't you?'

Ameera laughs a menacing laugh and Salma shakes her head laughing

Salma: You're such a bitch! I knew you would bring that up! And you *always* get it wrong. YOU pissed yourself, I shat myself.'

Ameera is laughing hysterically now.

Ameera; 'Oh yeah, you did a massive poo didn't you?'

Salma pushes Ameera playfully whilst still roaring with laughter and makes various threats about spilling her embarrassing moments.

Salma: 'What about the time you pissed the bed? There was so much wee, everyone had to take the mattress into the garden and wash it, mum and dad *and* the neighbour! Or what about the time dad was cutting your nails and he picked up the bits he had cut and smelt them, pulled a face, looked at you and gave you a massive slap?'

Hysterical laughing continues between both sisters, Ameera is trying to get a word in but Salma is on the rampage now. She tries to put her hand over Ameera's mouth in an attempt to stop her talking and to allow her to continue telling the story.

Salma: 'It was because he could smell shit! You had been scratching your bum and he could smell shit.'

Both girls are in complete hysterics now and even I'm laughing with them. Slowly they compose themselves, the laughter dies down and is replaced by huge grins.

Ameera: 'It's true, it's true, I don't mind saying it. This is anonymous so I don't care! I did wet myself at the mosque. It was after the *maulvi* said my pronunciation was crap and so I would have to read again after the girl next to me had read. If my pronunciation was still wrong at that point then the stick with the nails would be saying hello to my palms. I couldn't stop myself, I was too scared to ask to go to the toilet and too scared to move so I just went whilst sat there. The girl next to me on the floor, I think she was called Sophia or something like that, was the first to notice. The wee started to form a pool and move towards her until it touched her feet, I watched the whole thing happen in slow motion....Sophia screamed 'Oh my gaaaaaawwwddd, she's done a piss'. I think the *maulvi* was so disgusted, he didn't even bother to hit me.'

Salma: (still laughing) I remember when Sophia shouted that, I felt bad for you. The *maulvi* didn't hit you but mum gave you a good slap, right across your face when I took you home didn't she?'

Ameera nods at Salma, still laughing.

Ameera: 'I know we laugh and joke about it a lot but why did you poo yourself?'

Ameera is trying hard not laugh. Salma looks at her smirking and shakes her head

Salma: 'I don't know to be totally honest. My stomach wasn't bad or anything, I think I thought I needed to fart but instead did a poo. It was more embarrassing for me because the *maulvi* made me go home with the poo still in my knickers.'

Ameera starts to laugh again

Ameera: 'Sorry, sorry, I won't laugh anymore, it's just one of those memories that makes me laugh whenever I think about it. How cruel was it though that the *maulvi* didn't let you go the bathroom to clean up? It was pretty harsh making me take you home to face mums wrath instead.'

Salma: 'Mosque was pretty hard-core wasn't it? I remember one of the *Maulvi's* used to hit that girl, Sabeena Patel, you remember her? She used to stink of piss, they used to always hit her behind her legs so she would fall to her knees and then hit her back with that pipe. She was so daft, remember how she would skive off mosque and instead of going somewhere far away, she would skive off to play with her brother outside the fucking mosque!'

Ameera: 'Do you not think she had a disability or something? Whenever I think back to her, I think Asperger's. I felt really sorry for her. She couldn't talk very well either could she? She used to skive off mosque and sit in this bit of grass, right in front of the mosque and pick flowers with her younger brother. I don't think she actually made conscious decisions to skive off, I think she just wanted to pick flowers and didn't understand why she couldn't do that. Same with that boy, the one with the lazy eye that the *maulvi* bought in one day and kicked the shit out of.'

Salma: 'Oh god, yeah I had forgotten about that. I wonder what he had done to deserve that beating?'

Ameera looks directly at me. All the smiles have gone.

Ameera: 'The *maulvi* brought this boy into our class one evening, we had about 20 minutes to go until home time. I say he brought him into our class, what I mean is that he threw the boy into our class. Our class was in a basement so there were about 6 steps you had to climb down to get to the classroom. This boy was pushed right from the door and so he tumbled down them into a heap at the bottom. The *maulvi* then just started to kick the shit out of him. He had his pipe to hand and was just smacking this boy, smacking him full force all over his body. He got tired of using the pipe so threw that down and started to push, pull, punch and kick him instead. He would get the boy to stand on his feet and then start punching, kicking and kneeing his stomach until he fell to the floor. The boy always looked on the verge of tears but didn't cry. The *maulvi* kept screaming 'You're so clever aren't you? You think you're so clever you bastard.' I don't know how he took that beating, it must have gone on for about 5 minutes, just punches, kicks and elbows. I can't remember the boys name but I can still see his face, clear as anything. I think he had a learning disability of some kind, he was really slow, couldn't talk much and didn't know when he was supposed to say something and when he wasn't. You know how you get autistic people sometimes who just say things as they are and take meanings to be literal? Well he was like that. Sometimes when I really, deeply think about him, Sabeena and others at mosque, including us two, I get really upset. The memories upset me enough still to make me cry.'

Salma: 'That *maulvi* was a fucking dickhead, an absolute dickhead. I think you're right, that boy had some sort of learning difficulty. I don't know.'

There are a few second of silence as the sisters digest this memory.

Ameera: 'Hey you do you remember the mosque library? I remember that so-called library in the mosque! I remember how excited I was when they opened it and we were allowed to borrow books. I don't know what I was expecting in terms of genre, I think I thought it would be like the school library but it wasn't. It was full of Islamic books. I didn't sleep for months after reading some of them, especially the one about the Djinns.'

Salma: 'Oh gosh I remember that, you wouldn't sleep with the lights switched off for months, and you would cover all the mirrors. I remember you cried a lot. Did you wet the bed? I think I can remember you wetting the bed.'

Salma smirks

Ameera: 'Yeah I did, lots of times. You shouldn't laugh! I was petrified. The book about Djinns was bad but I also remember reading the one about grave punishments and what you could expect if you did certain things. If you cut your hair as a woman, you could expect to be strangled by metres and metres of black hair, it would go down your throat and through your eyes and nose, continuously until the Day of Judgement. If you wore nail varnish you would have your nails ripped off over and over again until the Day of Judgment arrived. I remember reading the story about the man who was tearing flesh from his brother's back and then eating mouthfuls of it! It was a punishment for backbiting and gossiping about someone behind their back. There were these stories about the most disgusting things that would happen to the women who had pre marital sex. It was frightening to be a woman. You couldn't do *anything*. Listening to music had a punishment, dancing had a punishment, drinking alcohol had a punishment, gossiping had a punishment, having a vagina had a punishment- women couldn't do anything!'

The sisters turn to ask me if I know about Djinns, I tell them the truth which is I know very little.

Salma: 'They are beings, like us, but are created from fire as opposed to mud and clay. They live with us, alongside us, but in another sort of dimension. They can see us and hear us but we can't see or hear them. Djinns and humans are strictly forbidden to interact with each other and enter each other's worlds. There are some really pious men in the world who are able to talk to the djinns and even control them. There are cases of humans becoming possessed by djinns and being made to do all kinds of things. There also stories about djinns marrying humans…you *have* to believe in djinns if you are a Muslim, it's like a must have belief to be a Muslim, a pre-requisite. Also, they can travel huge distances in seconds and can cross continents in seconds. In fact, you know that magician David Blaine? Well, lots of people in the Asian community are convinced that he has control of a Djinn and that's how he does some of his crazy tricks….It was scary reading that stuff but I wasn't as affected as Ameera, I just didn't think about it much. Until Haleema got possessed by one.'

Ameera: 'Bloody hell, totally forgot about her and that episode.'

Salma: 'Haleema was one of our closest friends growing up and we would all play together at her house. She was the only girl in her house with 4 brothers so we were like sisters to her. We used to play dress up in her mum's old clothes and bake rubbish cakes. Her mum and dad were really nice and really well thought of within the community. They were religious people and really well respected. One evening, dad came back from the mosque and told us all that Haleema had been possessed by a djinn. There was a big push from the mosque to try and cleanse her of the djinn and save her. I remember dad was really scared and left the house that night to go to Haleema's house and help with the exorcism. We don't know what happened that night but we never played together again did we?'

Ameera: 'No we didn't. I remember Dad crying after he came back from Haleema's and saying things like 'I have seen the devil tonight.' For the next few weeks, we would go to her house and ask for her so we could play together but her mum and dad would say she wasn't well. We saw her about a year later leaving her house. She spoke to us and said she was moving to London to get married – she was 14. She was very stony faced and expressionless, I remember thinking that. And we never saw or heard from her again. I assume she is still in London, I don't know. Her mum and dad sold their house and moved to London too. I can still see her face though. I can remember her laugh and remember the clothes we used to dress up in. I can even remember the smell of her house and the basement we would play in. Dad said that Haleema had been on her period and walking back at dusk, alone, past a building site, a favourite haunt for Djinns and that's why she was possessed by one. You're also not allowed to enter a graveyard after sunset or dusk as a woman because you are likely to get possessed by a djinn. You are not to frequent a long list of places when you are menstruating because this leaves you vulnerable to a djinn. It scared me senseless. I kept thinking there were djinn's watching me, following me and trying to possess me. It stopped me doing quite a lot, like singing whilst sat on the toilet or locking the door in the bathroom so I could dance - toilets were another favourite haunt of the Djinn.'

Salma: 'I didn't realise you thought so deep into it. I just accepted it as part of Islam and trusted they wouldn't harm me if I didn't bother with them. You don't even believe in the religion anymore, you have nothing to be scared of.'

Ameera: 'It still impacts you though, having something drilled into your head still impacts you. The whole Djinn thing formed my toilet habits. I hate being in there longer than I need to now. I don't visit graveyards either. It just sort of enters into your subconscious and stays there. Also mirrors, I hate mirrors in the dark. I try not to look at them in case I see something staring back. That sounds silly, there *will* be something staring back, me! I mean seeing someone else staring back at me. I know *you* believe in them Salma and believe that they can possess humans but I can't help thinking that poor Haleema might have just had a mental health problem. Like schizophrenia or something. And the men interpreted it as a possession. I hate thinking about it. I find it so desperately saddening. It made me not want to go anywhere after dusk. I was scared to sit under trees- another favourite haunt of the djinn. I even remember thinking I had better not look too nice because you can attract them that way too. I didn't wear makeup, leave my hair down, go anywhere in the evenings or get involved in the latest fashion trends because that could all attract a djinn too.'

Salma: 'It was all very controlling wasn't it? Everything controlled you or was supposed to, it shaped you…Do you remember the Bosnia video?'

Ameera: 'Yeah, that made me wet the bed too. I didn't sleep for months after watching that. How old do you think we were?'

Salma: '10 or 12, something like that. We were made to watch a video of the Bosnian war. It was a brutal, devastating war and there were murders of all creed of person including Muslim. Lots of Muslims were killed and some of the atrocities committed against the Muslims were really horrific. The mosque became involved because of the number of Muslims being killed and one evening in class, we were shown a grainy video. We could see piles and piles of bodies, naked men, women and children, cut limbs, dead eyes, burnt bodies and gory injuries. It was just so brutal. I think the tape was made by someone undercover, I can't be sure. We were told of the rapes of the men, women and children, and the babies. I remember feeling sick, I remember crying and feeling outraged that Muslims were being massacred like this. I remember feeling really angry at people for not doing anything. I remember thinking we Muslims need to stick together.'

The sisters continue to talk more about this video and the bodies on show. Once they felt there was nothing more to try and remember about the tape they fall silent. We sit in silence for close to sixty seconds until Ameera breaks the silence.

Ameera: 'You do remember the paedophile don't you? I know we never talk about it.'

Salma: 'Course I remember him. I remember every little thing.'

The sisters go on to explain their weekends and activities. There was no money to go on family trips out so they would forage in bushes and find things to play with. One of their favourite games to play was simply called shop. A pretend shop in which they would sell each other things such as smooth pebbles, shiny bits of glass they would find, big leaves, bright flowers. They would use two rocks as a pestle and mortar, grinding leaves until they resembled cooked spinach. This would be offered in their shop. When they were not playing shop, they would wander over to the 10 single wooden garages that stood, partly sheltered in tall unruly grass, trees and bushes. This site was due for demolition and would, a decade later, become a paved seating area, complete with an abstract sculpture. The wooden garages may have been large sheds; the sisters can't remember exactly but do remember calling them garages. All the garages bore the remnants of paint- blues, reds and greens, now peeling, faint and neglected. Some of the garages had large padlocks on them but the sisters have no recollection of what might have been inside. A number though, had no lock and housed stray cats, vermin, cigarette butts, used syringes and used condoms.

Ameera: 'I saw him first. I was playing with the other kids from our street between the garages, playing tag and hide and seek. He was old, probably in his 60's and looked like he slept rough. Obviously, I didn't think that when I first saw him, it was only years later when reflecting that I remembered his tatty clothes, his tatty hat and white beard. His brown tatty coat and his fingerless gloves. There must have been about 14 of us kids playing together, just running around screaming and shouting. We were all about seven or eight years of age. Some of the kids had formed a semi circle around him and when I heard someone shout 'sweets', I scurried across too. I don't know where Salma was at that point.

When I joined the rest of the kids, I saw the old man was the attraction. He was squeezing a pink thing in his hand near his crotch. We were all close enough to see that every time he squeezed, this whitish liquid came out from this pink thing. He was using his finger to collect the liquid and then offered it to us saying it was sugary and sweet. I saw some of the boys lick it from his finger and sort of say 'mmmmm' like kids do. I was queuing up for my taste when Salma, who had come from nowhere and was stood behind me, pulled me back and said 'No, don't touch that. Don't touch it. It's dirty, it's his willy.' A few of the others heard what she said and started to scream, point and laugh like kids do. Two younger boys didn't join in with the laughing and shrieking though, they carried on waiting to taste some more. This guy told the boys he had more at his house and the three left together. I didn't know the boys or their families. I don't know if any of the other kids ran and told the parents of these two boys that they had left with this *gora*. I don't know. It makes me sad to think about that even today. How close we were to our house and still, we had such a close encounter with a paedophile. I would have gone too, if Salma had not been stood behind me when I was lining up for a taste and hadn't pulled me back, I would have gone too. I don't know what happened to the boys. I never heard anything but I guess even if something did happen, the Asians are so good at keeping it quiet, we would never have found out.'

Salma: 'Sometimes I think all of that was a dream. I used to see him quite a lot, just hanging around the garages. We didn't play there again. We used to break into our school instead and play in the playground. I wonder if anyone ever cottoned onto what this old white man was doing, lurking in the bushes where all the Asian kids played? I mean, it was a totally Asian street. He must have been caught I think because having a *gora* around was so rare and people would have noticed it, like today. If a *gora* moved into the area where mum and dad live, everyone would know about it. I sometimes get a feeling that he was caught though, I don't know. If he was caught by the Asian men, they would have killed and buried him without a doubt.'

There is a silence between the sisters as they take in what they have discussed. Salma stares into empty space with her lips pressed firmly together. Ameera eventually breaks the silence

Ameera: 'Heyyy remember how we used to think beer was urine?'

Both girls start laughing again

Salma: 'Yeah, I remember thinking how dirty white people were. They eat pork and then drink large glasses of piss. I remember the adverts for Carling, whenever they would come on TV, Dad would spit at the TV.'

More laughter

Salma: 'Mum used to get so mad at him for spitting on the TV because she would have to clean it up! I think I was easily 13 or 14 years old before I realised that it wasn't piss but alcohol. We were so naïve! We would believe anything that mum and dad told us. I was so scared of *gorey*, mum would use it as a threat too. She'd tell me to shut up or the *gorey* would come to get me. I think I read somewhere that white people used to say that to their kids once. They would say that the black man would come and get them. Remember when we moved to Walnut Street, to the new council house? Mum was so happy. A brand new council house in a street full of other Asian families. There must have been 50 houses on the street and there wasn't a single white family. We were in our early teens then and white flight was really taking place. It's sad really because it would have created more harmony within the community if there was a better mix of backgrounds, like one big melting pot. The house was lovely. It was large enough for all of us and I remember for the first few years,

we used to enjoy washing up in the kitchen! Mum was so proud! She and ι
would go to the local car-boot sale every Sunday and pick up some new trinket
for the house. There was such a mish mash of colour and crap everywhere.'

*The house soon started to become old. The sisters discuss the ageing of the
house*

Ameera: 'No one taught mum how to properly clean a house in the west. She
came from a mud hut and never had to deal with tiles, grouting and mould. Dad
was in the same boat as her with understanding this. Their education levels are
extremely basic and they didn't understand damp and humidity or why the
bathrooms kept getting mould on the walls or the importance of ventilation. Do
you know what my mum still calls the extractor fans in the kitchen and
bathroom? Fans. She thinks they work like fans and blow air in. She doesn't
understand that they extract air out. I used to tell her to put the extractor on
when she was about to have a shower and she would say 'No, it's too cold!'

I used to get really annoyed with her a few years ago when I would visit and
stay the night. Mum would cook curries as though she was preparing for some
huge feast. She always goes way over the top whenever either of us visit home.
It's quite sweet really bless her. I would ask mum to keep the kitchen door
closed, the extractor fan on, and windows open but she wouldn't listen. I used
to stink of curry, my hair, my clothes- everything. What makes it worse is once
you've been in that environment for a few hours, you can't smell the curry on
yourself anymore. I always find that I think I smell ok until I get back to my
own home and smell my clothes - they stink! No wonder we have this
reputation of being smelly, what can you do when you can't even smell it on
yourself? The damn spices seep into everything, so even if you do change your
clothes before you go out somewhere, the smell is still there. It gets right into
the fabric and into my hair. So you end up in a house that reeks of curry and
damp, not a great combination.

I remember when we had a really hot summer, only a few years ago and we got
maggots in the bins. Mum was going mental, she honestly thought someone had
binned cooked rice without putting it into a bag first. Mum actually thought that
maggots were old, cooked rice grains coming to life. I remember trying to
explain to her that they were flies, as babies, but I don't think she believed me.
Then I remember the cockroaches. They were massive and they were
everywhere. All the houses on the street had them one summer. At night, whilst
lying in bed, I could hear them scuttling around, it was horrible. I remember
sitting in my room sometimes with the window open when the garbage men

p. ·

e the bins. I would hear them shout to their supervisor and
e shouldn't have to do this, its fucking disgusting. It's
ɪ and safety at risk.' Sometimes they wouldn't collect the
ĸs and we would get cockroaches again. I remember feeling the
ɪy cheeks, a mixture of embarrassment and anger whenever I
used to ᴉᴉᴄ. ᴉe bin men. Mum tried her hardest to keep the house clean and we
did a lot of the chores too. Mum and dad eat curry, that is their food so their
bins are never going to smell of flowers are they? They are going to smell of
old curry. It didn't help that the neighbourhood kids had absolutely no
discipline. They would just chuck their rubbish onto the floor regardless of
where they were. I guess for their parents, this was normal behaviour because
it's what you did in India. They didn't have bins everywhere so people just
threw their rubbish wherever they wanted. There still isn't a public bin where
mum and dad live so any kids that decide to come and play near their house just
throw their rubbish onto the floor. Poor dad goes out with a bag and collects it
all up.'

Salma: 'Yeah he *used* to pick up the rubbish but now the kids don't play there
anymore because dad made a sign and stuck it up outside the house saying 'no
ball games allowed' all in capitals. I laughed sc hard when mum told me this.
Apparently the neighbours complained to mum saying he can't do that and their
kids need somewhere to play. But dad being dad said the sign stays and no ball
games are allowed anymore. They are all scared of him or respect him or
something because they listened and that damn sign is still there. Dad now sits
beneath it, on his deck chair, enjoying the silence and no rubbish. The best one
though was when dad decided too many people were parking near the house so
he painted yellow lines right down the street.'

Both girls laugh and shake their heads

Ameera: 'You couldn't really blame him for the line painting scandal though
could you? There were so many Asian lads who would just park wherever the
hell they pleased with no regards for the people who actually lived on the street.
He added a sign saying 'resident parking only' too. I remember I was having a
rubbish time at work that day but could not stop laughing when I called home
and mum told me that. Dad really is a character though isn't he? Mum and dad
both had some really nonsensical views on things like personal hygiene and how
to live your life on a day to day basis. Mum still bathes once a week. Every
Friday, the holy day. She will shower and wash her hair. That's how it was
done in her village when she was a little girl. You would bathe after sex of
course but for the older lady, it was once a week. Bathing that is, not shagging.

Mum and dad would have a pop at us for showering daily or almost daily when we all lived together. We would get told off because of the associated cost of water. But as we grew older and they became accustomed to a more western life, they almost encouraged it. Dad still tells us to go and shower or have a long bath when we go to visit. They understand that showering everyday is normal not abnormal. Mum is better too but she still holds some daft views. She doesn't like us to shower whenever we are on our period, she says that wind could get 'up there' and cause illnesses.'

Salma starts to laugh whilst Ameera smiles and shakes her head

Salma: 'Mum has a simple thought process, blood is coming out therefore all the tunnels must be open and susceptible to an attack by who knows what? Germs? The wind? Mum had us believing that showering during our period was not the thing to do. We must have absolutely stunk. Well you did didn't you Ameera?'

Salma starts to laugh

Ameera: 'Yeah yeah, I was on work experience at a hospital and on my period. One of the nurses took me aside and asked me if I was on my period. I said yes I was and she then gave me a bottle of deodorant spray and said to have a wash in the ladies and use that because she could smell me. I wasn't too embarrassed because she was so nice about it to me but yeah, I must have absolutely stunk. Do you use tampons by the way?'

Salma: 'No, it makes me feel ill thinking about stuffing one of those up there. Why? Do you?'

Ameera: 'No, I feel a bit like you do. Isn't it weird though because they are more hygienic then pads. With pads, the blood just sits there pressed up against your bits. At least with a tampon it's all contained, discreet and you don't rustle when you walk. It's cultural, using towels instead of tampons. Tampons will break your hymen and then no one will marry you. Apparently. Heyyy remember that day you bought home your bag of goodies from school?'

Ameera starts laughing. It takes Salma a few seconds to latch onto what her sister is laughing at. Her face changes to a grin as she remembers.

Salma: 'Oh yeah you bitch, I know what you're laughing at. At school one day, we had a lesson on sex education, periods and stuff. We all got a bag that contained a tampon, a pad, a condom and a leaflet with instructions on how to use condoms, I think. I rushed home and showed it to mum. She was horrified and grabbed the whole thing from me with one hand whilst giving me a massive slap with her other! Right across my face! She binned everything in disgust except the pad, which she put into one of her drawers. Mum likens tampons to penises, for her 'pure girls don't use tampons.'

Ameera: 'Ha! If only she had known your purity was long gone.'

Both girls laugh

Salma: 'Piss off, I am pure. Anyway, I don't think I would ever use tampons, seeing them as being wrong is too deeply ingrained in me now. I used to get huge slaps right across my face from mum regularly. Like the time when I started my period. I had my hand down my pants whilst watching TV, don't ask me why I had my hand down my pants, I just did. Anyway, when I bought my hand up it had some blood on it so I sort of scream shouted to my mum 'MUUUUM LOOOOOOK IT'S BLOOOOD.' Of course, dad was also in the room and heard me so mum responded by giving me a huge slap across my face and dragging me upstairs. She gave me this fucking massive pad to put in my knickers and that was it. About a day later, mum asked me where I was binning my used pads. I told her I hadn't binned any…'

Ameera: (laughing hard) 'Stinky cow, I remember mums face when it dawned on her you had been wearing the same pad for over a day. It must have been so heavy.'

We are all laughing at this story. Neither Ameera nor Salma give me the impression that they are bitter towards their parents. I ask them some more around this

Ameera: 'I don't think we have the luxury of choice in this matter. As parents, they did the best they could with what they had. I don't just mean with love and money but with knowledge too. They tried to drill an alien culture into us. Some bits stuck and others didn't. As we got older and became more educated, we saw the cultural constraints for what they were and we learnt the power of the word no. I am pretty certain they regret allowing us to become educated. Mum and dad have said sometimes that education has spoiled us. It must be hard for them especially when all our female cousins have married their cousins, had arranged marriages, have children and keep their parents happy. We are a rarity in the community. I know that we are used as an example by other families, as the girls who got too educated and became too westernised. I wear what I want, I enjoy good wine and I eat whatever meats I want. I have had several long term partners, all white, and I am not ashamed of any of it. There are people within my own family who feel I'm a complete disgrace and have told me so. I'm sure my parents are tremendously embarrassed deep down but that's their issue. I try to be as accommodating and sensitive as possible to other people's beliefs and customs. I never rub my life into the faces of other people, particularly those people who have beliefs very different to mine. I always dress to cover my body whenever I visit home. I don't sit at the table with my dad eating a bacon butty and swigging from a bottle of whiskey! I am respectful and live by the 'what they don't know can't hurt them' rule. We could make out our early lives were abusive and neglectful, we meet the criteria according to the standards set in the western world but what's the point in that? I have closure for most things. I understand why mum, dad, the community, the men, the cousins, the *maulvi's* - I understand why all these people do what they do, why they did everything they did. They were and are scared of change. Scared of losing their culture, their position, scared of being mocked and ridiculed. It is such a patriarchal society and they keep women supressed. By 'they' I don't mean men, both men *and* women keep the women down. The community can be a complete bitch if you don't fit the mould or adhere to its rules.

I used to have a place in the community once and my cousins, friends, aunts and uncles loved me for being a good little Indian girl. Then I went to college and university and started seeing it for the patriarchal and oppressive place it is. I saw the way it shackles you and keeps the men on top. My illiterate mum can't read or write in her mother tongue or in English BUT, she can recite meaningless passages of Arabic from the Quran when she prays her *namaaz*. I wish that Dad had allowed mum to have driving lessons, English lessons – all the evening classes that were made available for the minorities for free. I wish dad had allowed mum to go to these places and have a little more freedom. I wish mum and dad could have the education I have had. I don't mean a masters or even a degree, just the basic stuff like GCSE's and maybe A-levels. It would be invaluable for them, to help them understand basics. We have wasted so much time trying to get them to understand basic things, basic body functions and things like that. Both our parents self-diagnose their medical problems. Currently mum has a huge stomach, its fat. She is fat. But she is convinced it is not fat. She is convinced that it is air trapped inside of her. She had to have a hysterectomy, that took over a year to get her to agree to it, and now she is convinced that because of this operation and the empty space that has been left inside her, she is full of air that has no-where to go.'

Ameera looks exasperated explaining. Salma is nodding along agreeing with her sister

Salma: 'It really did take us all over a year to convince mum to have the hysterectomy. She had been going back and forth to the doctors for about 2 years because of pains in her womb. She had cysts on her fallopian tubes and within her womb, the best thing for her was a hysterectomy. But mum was convinced it would stop her from being a woman. Other females from the community were telling her the same thing, to not have the operation because it would stop her being a woman! Even dad said that she should not have the operation because it is removing what makes her female. There was this insinuation that she should put up with the pain and continue to be a woman. Now that she has had the operation, she has gained weight but believes it is because she has a gap in her body, which is now full of air. This is on top of the other bits of nonsense she believes. One lady from the community told her, after prodding her huge belly, that it was stones. That mum had stones in her belly. Mum drank some sort of powdered husk that she was given by this woman to try and rid her of these 'stones' but it didn't work surprise surprise. There is so much of this rubbish that goes on within the community. The women self diagnose. I think the doctor became so sick of mum, her constant visits and her insistence that she had stones and therefore needed an x-ray that he eventually agreed with her. I remember how smug mum was when she told us how she had been right all along, how the doctor had agreed with her diagnoses of stones and advised her to drink the potion the lady had given her. She now has something else wrong with her, she is convinced it's heart trouble. Her favourite word at the moment is 'blood sugar'. Whenever she feels a little off colour, basically every day, she says her 'blood sugar' is low and proceeds to eat the sweetest thing she can find. Then she wonders why she is getting fatter.'

Ameera: 'More air is getting trapped inside her! The last time we were both at home, we watched her eat two mangoes, half a watermelon, 4 oranges and 3 bananas. I was telling her to not eat so much but she kept saying 'Oh it's fruit, it's good for you. There is nothing in fruit.' She doesn't understand that food, even fruit, has calories, carbohydrates and fats attached! She probably ate 1200 calories of fruit in one sitting! It wouldn't be so bad if this was the only thing she was eating but no, she then went on to have one chapatti and a small amount of curry. She kept saying she was having a tiny amount of curry so it didn't count but her curries are full of oil and butter! Even if she only has a small amount, it's still high in calories and fat. She has no knowledge on calorie content or fat content. She gets really confused when she carries on gaining weight even though she has only eaten fruit, small amounts of curry and a small chapatti. When the scales show weight gain, she becomes really despondent and goes back to eating chapatti and curry three times a day and gains *more* weight. She convinces herself, with the help of her friends, that she has done everything possible to lose weight and she is still fat therefore it's not fat in her body but something else. Something like stones. I feel really sorry for her. I know we laugh at her but it does seriously fuck me off. Why hasn't the doctor done something about her mental health? Why can't they be firm with her and tell her she is talking a load of nonsense? I'm going to answer my own questions here, it's probably because they don't know what to do with her. If it was you or me, we would be referred to a counsellor or a psychologist but where the hell do you start with mum? She can't speak the language and doesn't understand basic science. She is a lost cause. Ha ha Salma, I just remembered something. Remember when, years and years ago, she went to the doctor with some complaint about her toilet problems? The doctor gave her some tablets and asked her to bring in a urine sample in a weeks time? Mum went home and started to collect her sample, a week later she handed the doctor a 2 litre bottle of Lilt, full of piss.'

We all laugh

Salma: 'She was so embarrassed! She didn't realise she was supposed to leave the doctors room and pick up a small red top bottle from reception. She thought the doctor wanted her wee from the entire week. It makes me laugh when I think of her carrying the massive plastic bottle full of wee around with her.'

Ameera: 'Remember the mothballs being crushed and shoved into our hair as a cure for nits? She was trying to suffocate them by smell! My head hurt for what seemed like weeks, and I stunk of mothballs for months. Which bright spark told her that was a good idea? Remember dad dipping oranges in sugar? That's the only way he would eat them! He used to sprinkle sweetener on the apples too didn't he? And castor oil, she used to put that in our hair as a cure for nits too! Dad really is something you know. When I was there about two months ago, I stayed the night and he found me in the morning drinking coffee in the kitchen. It was about 6am but Dad was surprised to see me so early and thought I was ill. Once I told him that I get up early every day it's a habit, he stopped worrying and turned his attention to what I was drinking. He thought it was coke. It wasn't, it was black coffee and I explained to him that I liked my coffee black. He asked me if I had put sugar in and I told him no, I never added sugar to my black coffee. And that was it! His eyes started to fill up with tears and he put his arm around me and said, 'I knew you were strong but today you have shown me how strong you really are. You drink coffee without cream and sugar, I am very proud of you!' I was like what the fuck....ha ha ha. Dad thinks I am a strong person not because I broke free or have a career or juggle two cultures but because I can drink a fucking Americano. Ha ha ha bless him. Oh god Salma, do you remember Ramadan?'

Salma: 'Yeah, long days weren't they for us as kids? I used to like getting up between 2 and 3.00am to eat before the fast closed for the day. Dad would buy chocolate mousse pots for us all to eat which was quite a treat. That's probably the only reason I used to like getting up. I have little doubt that the chocolate mousse pots were a bribe from dad. If we agreed to fast, we could get up in the night and eat chocolate mousse! It never felt like the middle of the night though did it? Every house on the street would be awake and eating, the neighbours would come round to borrow something or even eat with us. There was a real sense of community wasn't there?'

Ameera: 'Those are fonder memories I have of us all together. I hated the fasting, especially at primary school during lunch time. I would get so hungry whenever the smell from the canteen would float towards us.'

Muslims across the globe fast for 30 days during the month of Ramadan. The fasts are there to remind Muslims of the hunger and suffering that millions live through on a day to day basis. It is common for children as young as 3 years of age to observe fasts during Ramadan, something which has sparked debates between parents, community leaders, health officials and teachers.

Salma: 'I definitely think it's better today because you have some of the more educated Asians who don't let their young kids fast. You're still developing at that stage so starving yourself every day for 30 days can't be good. It impacts your brain and stuff doesn't it? It must do, if you are going without food or water for what? 12 to 15 hours a day? It doesn't make sense for children to fast either. If you are truly religious and spiritual then you will observe Ramadan and understand *why* you are fasting. It should not be about losing weight or just doing the fasts because they are part of a religion. Nor is it about keeping a fast because you want to be seen as all grown up at the age of 5. We can all laugh at 5 year olds when they put on their mum's heels or dad's suit and walk around pretending they are adults but not when they are starving themselves and potentially causing damage. Fasting is about being able to understand and comprehend, to some extent, the starvation millions face every day. I know it's not the same as an actual starving person because somewhere in our head, we know that the fast will end in 12, 13 hours and we know we will have something to eat and be ok. I guess we won't ever know how someone who is actually starving feels, unless we are in the exact same position as them. After all, you can use your willpower and get through one day of not eating when you *know* there is food waiting for you at a given time. Whenever I fast, I think about these things. When my stomach aches because I have not eaten for a day, I think of those people who have not eaten for weeks and pray for them. I am so aware that what I do to remind me of their suffering, this fasting, isn't anything like the suffering that they actually face. To understand that, we would have to make sure we had no food for 30 days and no expectation of food to come. Maybe that way, we would begin to understand desperation and actual starvation. How can children be expected to understand all of that? If they can't understand it then they can't appreciate the reasons for fasting and if they can't do that, then they shouldn't be fasting at all.'

Ameera 'Ha ha, it still makes you mad doesn't it? Ha ha. I understand and agree with your view on the whole fasting thing though, I really do. But still, I feel like Ramadan has become something else now. It's not about remembering those less fortunate, it's more like something which we do every year because we are Muslims. Some of my friends link Ramadan to the nice food they get to eat every night when it's time to open your fast. Others link it to Eid celebrations and see Ramadan as just a period of hardship they have to face before they get to celebrate their Christmas - Eid. Every night during Ramadan when you open your fast is like being at a small party and Eid is one massive feast with presents, new clothes and money. Do you remember all the food that mum used to cook during Ramadan? There used to be about 5 different main dishes, lots and lots of fried things, cakes, sweets, buttery curries - I used to put weight on! It taught me how to gorge.'

Salma 'Hmm, I think it depends on you as a person, your own understanding of your religion and your spirituality. I think it would do a lot of good for a lot of people if they would stop, now and then, and remind themselves of *why* they are doing whatever they are doing. People lose focus don't they? Look at some of the Muslims today, like that Rochdale grooming gang. They called themselves Muslims and believed that they were Muslims but if they had stopped to actually ask themselves why they call themselves a Muslim, what *makes* them a Muslim, how a Muslim should live their life then they would never have thought it was ok to treat those white girls the way they did. It makes me feel ill thinking about that case and those poor girls. And that grooming gang in Oxford too. What the fuck is wrong with some of these people? I remember the media picking up on the fact that so many were Pakistani and asking whether there was a link. The police were all like 'No no there is no link' but there clearly is. I wish the influential people within the community would stand up and say 'Yes, there is a fucking problem here.'

Ameera: 'I think there is a problem. I think Pakistani and Indian men do target white girls but I don't think this has any link to religion. I think the link is a mixture of the caste of the men and their culture. They were all quite low caste weren't they? Dirty little fuckers. I remember the Asian lads at school used to talk about practising on a *goree* and marrying a *desi*. That was really normal to hear, cheeky bastards, assuming that I was going to sit there, like a good little Asian girl, waiting to experience my first shag when *they* decided it was time to. I think there is massive problem in the Asian community. I use Asian now to mean Indian, Pakistani, Bengali and that whole region. I think there is a massive problem with sexual abuse, sexual exploitation, domestic violence, financial and emotional abuse but no one wants to talk about it. The sexual abuse is rife, no one wants to acknowledge that it is happening though. It's really normal in parts of India, Afghanistan and Pakistan for men to have young boys as their first sexual experience- that's abuse! It's paedophilia but no one wants to talk about it. The amount of child sexual abuse that goes on in India is crazy. We, in this country, are only just hearing about the odd incident that the western media picks up on. Growing up, there were always these hushed rumours about some little girl being abused. There was even that case, do you remember? That case of that Indian greengrocer who got the shit kicked out of him before being chased out of our area after it was discovered he was sexually abusing Asian boys. We definitely have community justice don't we? Well, that's what the hard-core Asians will tell you but no one grants justice to the kids that are abused do they? They just pretend that nothing happened or expect you to be ok because they got the bastard who abused you!

India as a country makes me laugh. They have all these female goddesses and want to show the world how advanced they are with their technology and their education levels. They want to impress you with the fact that people now read Danielle Steel and 50 shades of Gray yet the influential people there, the majority of them male, want to keep the horrific stories of gang rapes quiet from the world. They have a problem. They have a huge problem, but maybe they don't want to end up being known as another South Africa where they estimate that half of the female population will experience sexual abuse in their lifetime. How shocking is that statistic? *Half of all women.* Just take that in. In India, child brides are still normal, they haven't got to where we are yet, where children are revered, protected and given a childhood. If she can bleed then she can breed! The woman is still seen as second class and that's not exclusive to Indian Muslims, the Hindu's are the same even though the Hindu religion preaches equality. All these cases of gang rapes and child rape in India, those arseholes were Hindu but no one is talking about the 'Hindu problem' are they? Argh! It makes me mad! Another huge gripe I have is Bollywood. Bollywood has so much to answer for. The films today still portray the woman as a second class citizen, as someone who *needs* a man, who *needs* marriage and children. The biggest grossing films in Bollywood have a tendency to be those centred around family life, hierarchy, culture and tradition. I don't watch the films anymore, I got sick of seeing too many females who were singing, dancing, love sick, attempting suicide because they couldn't marry their love. Then overcoming whatever the barrier was and living happily ever after, cooking and cleaning as the perfect wife and daughter in law. And the way these films portray career women! I wish I could watch one with you and show you Aisha, I really do. One of the last ones I saw was this pathetic film with this demure Indian girl who was the perfect daughter who covered her head, smiled shyly, looked down when men spoke to her, cooked, cleaned and everything else that good women are supposed to do. She married this business man who was nice and life was great until he started working with another Indian woman, a career woman! This career woman had a degree, drove a car and would brazenly look at the husband and other men right in their eyes. She would also wear revealing clothing, laugh loudly, drink alcohol and scoff at Indian traditions whilst speaking English- I kid you not. It goes on, she was shown to berate the simple wife, laughing at her for not wearing makeup. Or the latest fashion or not understanding English. And the good little Indian wife, didn't say anything back to this career woman, just looked forlorn and hurt and all helpless. Yes, I am being completely serious. Anyway, the demure wife has to compete for her husband's attention from this whore career woman who is trying to get her claws into the husband. The film ends with the career woman running off with another man, because after all, career women are sluts with loose morals. The husband begs his wife to forgive his foolishness and they all live happily ever after blah blah blah just kill me now.'

Salma laughs at Ameera as she collapses in a dramatic position onto the table and puts her head into her arms in an exasperated fashion. She is laughing too.

Salma: 'That's one of her soapbox rants- Bollywood! She hates Bollywood. I think the problem with the Asian men and the white girls does exist. Sometimes I see these *freshy's* that turn up and their eyeballs pop out of their sockets when they see western women, white women, walking around in skirts or shorts or going out and getting drunk, having boyfriends and sex. I think that they think 'I want a piece of that.' Remember, back in India, Pakistan and Bangladesh, it's totally different. In most of these south Asian countries, women don't show their body in public, they don't show their arms in sleeveless tops never mind have boyfriends or pre marital sex- well, not in public anyway. So when you go from that environment to this environment, where women have more equality and power, it must overwhelm them. Pornography has a lot to answer for too.

The porn available to these idiots abroad is western porn and shows western white women as willing to do *anything*. Willing to do *anything* and enjoying having *everything* done to them. The culture and religion also teaches that the virtuous woman is the virgin, who is respectful, who covers her modesty, covers her body, her hair, doesn't make brazen eye contact with men and so on. The woman who talks loudly, looks men in the eye, shows her body and dances and laughs is the harlot. All the white women they see out and about will be harlots to them. And harlots to them are fair game. It's not just the white women that are targeted though, Asian girls who *do* have boyfriends, go drinking, have sex are doubly disadvantaged. They get singled out for the same sort of grooming but they never report it because of the shame attached. I know too many friends from high school who had older Asian men chasing them at 13 and 14, forcing them to have sex and promising them marriage before dumping them. The girls do nothing because they are scared of the repercussions they will face from their own families for having a boyfriend in the first place. Asian boys target these girls and use them for sex knowing full well that they can shag and dump them because the girl can't tell anyone. If she does, her family will punish her first, her community second and then via the guilt that comes from her religion, she will punish herself. The girls I know who had to suffer this sort of treatment went one of two ways. They either found religion and became repentant, *hijab* wearing Muslim women or went the complete other way and carried on being used and spat out by men. It is so sad to see. There was a case recently in our home town where Asian girls in care were being targeted by Asian men. That stuff doesn't even hit the headlines. The grooming gangs are nasty, vicious bastards and it's those sorts of guys that make me think capital punishment should be brought back. But the important thing to remember is that you get vicious bastards that groom girls in all cultures. I don't think it is a Pakistani or Indian or 'Asian' problem, grooming girls that is. I think there is a problem though and that problem is Indian, Pakistani, Bengali, 'Asian' men *using* white girls and generally, vulnerable females. Having them as girlfriends but having absolutely no intention of marrying them. Scheming to shag vulnerable girls-White, Asian, Black whatever colour or creed without any intention of settling down with them. Just using them for their own physical pleasure and binning them when they have had their fill.'

Ameera: 'Yup, totally agree with you. The grooming isn't an Asian man problem but using white girls is. It is so common to see white girls get with Asian guys but so rare to see these Asian guys marrying those same white girls. Where they do, the girls have to convert and adopt a completely different way of life. I don't agree with that. That's a load of bollocks. If you love someone then you love *them*. Not their religion, what they wear, what they eat or what they worship. You love *them* and everything about them that makes them the person they are. Why can't they get married and each of them keep their own faith? I know there is the issue of children, and how to raise them, but why not teach the child about both of your beliefs so that when the kid is older, they can make a decision themselves? There is something really wrong with indoctrinating children. Is that naïve? I don't care if it is! I don't like it, it makes me feel uncomfortable thinking about instilling a load of alien values into an unknowing child. Religion for me, sorry Salma you won't like this, but religion for me has got a lot to answer for. As do the Asian men who sleep with white girls then break their hearts when they marry an Asian girl. And the poor Asian girl who tends to be fresh off the boat, she has a life where she has to live in the shadows and just accept that her husband will be out and about, living his life with white girls. It's us women, we are the ones that suffer, regardless of our colour or race or religion or culture, *we* are the ones that suffer. I can't wait for feminism to take root in this culture and empower women to stand up together against this bullshit.'

Salma: 'It's not the religion that causes the issue, it's the people who interpret it wrongly. Women are equal to men in Islam and....'

Ameera interrupts Salma

Ameera: 'But they're not though are they? You are fed a lie and told you are equal in the home. You are told that you are the head of the house as a woman and equal to your husband. That was probably all good and well in the days where our clans wandered the deserts and the men went out to hunt whilst the women cleaned the tents but in life today, we can't just exist in the home, we want to go out and work and have a life of our own. We want to have a say in our life, our futures and a say on what *we* think. It...'

This time Salma interrupts Ameera

Salma: 'If you would just shut up and listen to me for a minute Ameera! The Quran for me is all about interpretation and making sure it is in line with the world we live in today. For me, women *are* allowed to work and *are* equal to men in Islam. The man is supposed to help the woman in the home and in life in general. He is *supposed* to treat her with respect and *supposed* to split everything equally with her. The men that understand the religion and practise it correctly have really happy lives and happy marriages. When I went to Turkey, I met so many Muslim couples that identified as practising Muslims but the women were wearing skirts, sleeveless tops, makeup and even drinking beer! I managed to chat with one of these couples and they would answer my questions about things like the *hijab* with answers like how silly it was to wear a *hijab* in the blistering Turkish heat! One of the guys I spoke with said that he enjoyed a beer to cool down and as far he was concerned, Islam prohibited drinking alcohol because it can intoxicate you and make your lose your judgement so his rationale was that he liked a beer but never drank to get drunk. He interpreted the religion to suit him, not sure if I agree with his take on alcohol but to be honest who cares? As long as he is living his life as a good, kind and honest person then who cares? It's like my old school friend Rehana, how happy is she with her husband? They are both practising Muslims and treat each other so well. It *can* be done. You just get the idiots who misinterpret the religion for their own reasons or because they are just plain stupid. It doesn't help matters when you see that the only coverage the media want to show is that of the fanatics who make their wife's walk behind them and blow shit up. I wish they would show normal Muslim people more on TV.'

The sisters continue to discuss this point a little longer and then look to start wrapping this conversation up.

Ameera: 'You know that mum will ask you about marriage again when we go home?'

Salma: 'Yup, I am mentally ready for her now. I'm going to tell her to shove it. I am not getting married. I am not ready for it so if she wants to cry then she will just have to sit there and cry. She can only cry and rant for so long.'

Ameera: 'Well if it gets too much then we can just leave for a few hours, let her cool down. We can go out and grab a coffee somewhere and bring back some cake for her. A nice slab of cake will keep her quiet for a while.'

Both girls laugh and start talking to me about a new cake that is being sold in a coffee chain and how delicious it is. They bicker over the caloric content of this new cake and suggest that all three of us visit the coffee house for a slice each. And so we do.

3 PARVEEN

'No, I have never worked in this country, how could I? I can't even speak the language, who will give me a job?'

Parveen is a 34 year old Pakistani woman who arrived in the UK for a holiday about 7 years ago accompanied by her husband Rizwan and three young sons. Rizwan's brother, Rashid, was already settled in England with his British Pakistani wife and children. During their holiday to the UK, Parveen came to realise that they were really there to 'disappear'. Rizwan went on to America leaving Parveen and the children in England to claim asylum. I ask her about her arrival to the UK.

'It wasn't my decision to come here for a holiday, it was Rizwan's. His brother Rashid was already settled in the UK after marrying Shanaaz, our uncle's daughter. Shanaaz was born in the UK so Rashid's visa and residency was straightforward enough once they had married. But once Rashid got here, got a job, money, cars and a house, Rizwan decided that he wanted the same life as his little brother. Whenever Rashid would visit Pakistan he would always bring lots of gifts for people, lots of money was on show and he had his very own *Kothi* built in Pakistan too. The *Kothi* was huge and on three storeys, everyone from the village came to have a look at it. I think Rizwan was a bit jealous of Rashid. He had been working for years in all different countries like Qatar, Saudi Arabia, Malaysia and Dubai but had not made enough money, not like Rashid. That's what he kept telling me anyway, that the jobs in all the Arab countries did not pay him enough to stay in one country and build a life so he had to keep moving onto better opportunities. I don't know what his dealings were or how much money was going to be enough money for him. These *Rajahs,* their greed is like a bottomless pit. Rizwan came back to Pakistan from a stay in Dubai and immediately started on plans to get to America but there were some problems. I don't know the ins and outs of it but he had to get a green card or something and could only do that by working *in* America. I heard from him that he could only go to work in America if there was a job waiting for him, I think. Like I said, I can't be sure because I only heard bits from him and I was never involved in all the details. I couldn't really advise on anything because I didn't know anything about countries like America and England. I didn't even know what he was planning but I did say one thing to him. I told him I was not going to stay in Pakistan whilst he went off *again* and if he did that to me, if he left me and the children again, then I would not let him back. My mum backed me up on this too and told him the same. In Pakistan, it felt as though he was abroad all the time, I felt like a whore. He would come back for a few weeks, sleep in my bed, leave me with some money and then go off to another country again. I went through my pregnancies with my mum, went to the hospital with my mum and gave birth to each of his sons with my mum supporting me. He was always away in some country. He did come back though, after each child was born, he came back from whichever country he was in to see me and his new son.'

I ask her questions around her village, her family and life before she was married. I ask her what it was like when Rizwan would leave her for months at a time.

'Life before I was married? Well it was better! I tell you, don't get married and if you do, marry one of these *gorey*, they treat you better than the Asian men. That's one of the biggest things I have noticed in this country, just how free all the *goree's* are. And some of the Asian girls, I see how free they are and sometimes think how my life would have been if I had been born in this country and not in Pakistan. I grew up in a large family, my dad was Rizwan's uncle and so it was decided when I was really young that Rizwan and I would be married. I didn't mind so much, he was the gentlest out of all his brothers and everyone called him the wise one. Dad died of a heart attack at 52 years of age and the extended family turned their back on us. Dad had 5 brothers and 4 sisters who are all extremely wealthy. My grandfather was very rich and made money from land and farming in Pakistan. He had managed to get hold of a lot of land during the partition. Once he died, the money, houses and land all passed down to the brothers including my dad. Whilst dad was alive, we were all well looked after. We had our own fields on which we would grow whatever we could and made a very good living. When dad died, the brothers took my dad's land and split it between all the remaining brothers and sisters. It was the way things were done, there was no right to anything for my mum and she is still really bitter about it. And why shouldn't she be? I hate the way we were treated because we were girls. They decided we sisters would get married earlier and take the burden of looking after us away from mum. They took the decision away from Mum. They didn't even consult with her. I don't get on with my mother in law, Rizwan's mum, also my aunt as she was dad's younger sister. It was strange calling her aunt when we were children and then having to call her mum once I married Rizwan. She didn't like any of the wives her brothers had chosen and was pretty much nasty to all of them including my mum. There were always petty fights where my mum and my aunt would throw accusations at each other over the smallest of things. My aunt once accused my mum of causing dad's heart attack and therefore causing his death, I could never forgive that. How can anyone forgive that? It got worse and worse and eventually mum and my aunt started to hit and throw stones at each other. They were all so horrible to my mum. They had forcibly taken all the land away from my old mum and would give her a few rupees a week to spend. It was humiliating. My dad was the eldest out of all the brothers and sisters so all the land the family owned was his first! It should have passed to his wife when he died but the brothers took it all saying it was their families land and they would re share it out amongst the remaining brothers and sisters. My mum got nothing. We got nothing. Whilst dad was alive, we were all part of the bigger family but once he had gone, we were nothing to them really. Mum didn't have any sons, just girls, so there was no one who could inherit anything. If I had brothers then we would have been treated differently. If any of sisters had been living here in England then we would have been treated differently. Instead, all us sisters had to marry the sons of one of my uncles or aunties and that was our fate, our *kismet*. I was luckier than my sisters, my eldest sister had to marry Rizwan's older brother who is the village idiot and my younger sister married my other aunts' son who regularly beats her. Mum had to fight to make sure that I *did* marry Rizwan, because when the time came, my mother in law did try and wriggle out of it. She wanted Rizwan to marry the daughter of my other uncle, who was already in England so Rizwan could become settled in England. Anyway we got married and he was really kind to me at the start, really gentle.

He left after spending a few months to work in Saudi Arabia and would send money back to me and to his mum. The first arguments we would have were around this issue of money. I didn't understand why he needed to send anything to his mum when she was so wealthy anyway. The money he was sending me was keeping me, the children *and* my mum but he didn't care about my mum. After I had my first son, he came back for a few weeks and then went on to Qatar and it kept happening like this. He would visit me after I had given birth and then leave. He carried on sending money to me but never really spent time with me, as my husband. I thought he wanted to be away from all of the noise, fighting and the stress of the families. Mum and my aunties would fight almost daily. Our houses are all next to one another's and they would trade insults over the mud walls separating the front courtyards. I stuck up for my mum, I hate the way they treated her. The way we were all treated once dad had died. Rizwan and I were fighting all the time as the years went on. Some weeks he would not even bother to call me because we would end up fighting over the phone. His mum would find out that I had shouted at him or called him a name or something else and she would march over to my mum's house to tell me off and that would be it then. *Bas.* Mum and my aunt would start fighting again. It was just constant shouting, swearing and fighting. Eventually Rizwan's brother Rashid, got in touch and said he was organising a holiday for us in England. He said we would all travel there as a family and live with them for a few weeks and have a nice relaxing holiday. We all came here on a visitor's visa. Rizwan had a lot of documents with him that showed bonds worth thousands and thousands of pounds in his name. I asked him why he had all those documents and he told me that we had to show that we were only coming to the UK for a holiday and were not going to claim benefits. Anyway, we got to England and I met my eldest uncle, his wife auntie Rabia, and all their children. My uncle looked a lot like my dad, I cried when I first saw him and again when he hugged me. I had another uncle in England too but I didn't get to meet him until a few days after. I felt sorry for auntie Rabia, they treated her like they treated my mum, like she was nothing and only there to cook, clean and serve. I got along very well with her and her eldest daughter Shanaaz. People were surprised that me and Shanaaz got along so well considering we were sisters in law, I think they thought we would always be fighting but it wasn't like that for us. She was like a little sister to me. After a few days of being here, Rizwan and Rashid both told me together that Rizwan was leaving for America where he had found a job. I went crazy at him. I tried to hit him but his brother held me back. I just couldn't believe that he could do this to me again. And to his sons! My poor little boys would always ask after their father, they would always want to know when he was coming back. Whenever he returned from a trip abroad, they would ask me if he was going to stay for good this time. It's not fair on the children and it's not fair on me. So when he announced this time he was going to America I was so angry. Eventually I just sat down and cried. I didn't even know what else to do. I was surrounded by members of his family and they wouldn't even let me be angry. We had been married for 5 years and we had not spent more than 6 months together, what sort of marriage was this? Was kind of life was this?'

Parveen, Rizwan and her children arrived into the UK in 2010. They were greeted at the airport by Rashid with whom they would also be staying for the next few weeks. She tells me what happened during this time.

'Rashid's wife Shanaaz was really nice. I felt sorry for her. She had 7 girls, no boys and spent her whole day working, running after the children, cooking or cleaning. Shanaaz worked in a shop part time, but everything was so rush rush for her, not like it was in Pakistan. There you had plenty of time to do things but here it was just so different. The girls would get up early, she would dress them, feed them and get them all to school. Shanaaz would then go to work, and once that was finished, she would rush to pick the children up from school, feed them and then get them all to mosque. Once the children had left for mosque, Shanaaz would clean the house and cook something for dinner and then finally at night she would clean up after everyone had eaten and put the girls to bed. This is what it was like for her every single day. I tried to help her by cooking the evening meals and washing the plates when I could but things were still so busy for her. I didn't like the weather when I first came here. It was always cold or raining and I was miserable. My children were ok though, they would play with their new cousins and their new electronic toys. Rashid and Rizwan would often talk to each other at night, away from me and Shanaaz. I always wondered what they talked about.

It was Shanaaz who told me that I would be leaving with the kids soon and going to a house of my own. When I asked Rizwan about this, he said it was true and also told me he had booked his ticket to America and would be gone in a few days. He was looking at me sheepishly whilst he told me. At one point I thought he was laughing at me but he just kept saying he was nervous at what my reaction might be. Of course, I was very upset and called him every name I could think of. Once I had calmed down and stopped crying, he told me he was doing this for his family and for all of us but inside, I felt something was wrong. I suspected he had other wives and I asked him this but he denied it. I made him swear on the Quran, I made him swear that he didn't have any other wives. I made him swear that he was not planning on getting married again and he took oath after oath for me. He swore on my life and the lives of our children. I felt better about him leaving after that. Rashid and Shanaaz took us to Birmingham where there was a small dark house waiting for us. There were 2 rooms downstairs, 2 bedrooms upstairs, 1 kitchen, 1 bathroom and a small garden made of stone. The house smelt funny and there were dark stains on some of the walls. I hated it from the moment I stepped into it. There were a few pieces of old furniture; 2 beds, a sofa and some drawers. They told me that I would have to live in that house with the children who would be enrolled in a local school. They said they would send money to me to keep me going and I would only have to do this for a few weeks. I was terrified, I had no idea where anything was, I couldn't speak any of the language and I was far away from Shanaaz too. Rashid said that he would come to visit me and the children and that I should not worry. Rizwan said the same things as his brother. He told me I was strong and that I was able to do this. We spent the next few hours walking around the streets, finding the local shops and the shopping centre. We walked to the school that Rizwan said the children would go to and we bought supplies for the house. We all stayed in that little house that night. Shanaaz helped me to clean the house and make it smell better. We re-arranged some of the furniture and she helped me to cook a meal for everyone. The next morning we went out again to look at the shops, the school and to try and remember where everything was. Later that day Rashid, Shanaaz and the girls left to go back to their home. It was just me, Rizwan and my 3 boys left. We lived together for about 2 weeks as a proper family. It was one the best times of my life. We were an actual family. I asked Rizwan whether the children would be starting school soon but he told me that this would only happen once he went to America. We ate together as a family and we walked around Birmingham nearly every day. I started to know the area a little better and found where all the Asian shops were that sold spices and halal meat. Rizwan would keep telling me that I *had* to do this, that I *had* to make sure I did exactly as I was told so we could be a family together quicker. He said once he got his citizenship, he would call over my mum and she could live with us, away from his mother and all the shouting of Pakistan. I felt so happy that he was trying to help my mum. I thought he could finally see that they had all been unfair to her and unfair to me.

When Rashid and Shanaaz came a second time, I knew that Rizwan would be leaving with them. When they had all left, I felt so alone. I just sat on the floor with my children around me and sobbed. Those first few days were very bad for me but after a week or two had passed, I got myself through the sad times by thinking of the future and how we would all finally be a family *with* my mum here too. Rashid had introduced me to an elderly Asian man who lived nearby and had said that I should do everything the old man asks me to do and in return, he would look after me and my children. The old man was kind and he would often come with his wife or daughters to check that we were ok. Sometimes, he would even bring food for us all. Rizwan left me some money to keep me going for the next 2 months and I had Rashid's phone number if I needed anything urgently. The old man told me that some people would be visiting soon and would ask me questions. He said all I needed to say to them was I didn't speak English and to point at him and so I did as I was told. This happened a few times and different people visited, checking me and the children. The old man wouldn't tell me what was going on for a while but eventually, when I got upset thinking they were sending me away, he told me that these *gorey* thought I was here because I had nowhere else to go. I told the old man that he was mistaken and that I *could* go back to Pakistan but he laughed and said if I admitted that, they would send me back straight away and that's not what Rizwan wanted. He told these people that we had arrived here on holiday but my husband had left me and I was alone with nowhere to go. He told them I had no family in Pakistan and it was dangerous for me and my children to return. This was all so I could stay in England. I didn't know what I could do or what I should do so I did as they told me and kept quiet. I didn't even know how this was helping Rizwan in America but I did as Rizwan asked me to do before he left and I listened to the old man. My children started the school down the road and I started to receive some money every week from the government. It was about £60 per week and was supposed to be for the children. The house was paid for by the council and I received some more money because I did not have a job. In total I used to get about £100 per week to buy food, clothes and anything else that I or my boys needed. I also had to save some money to give to Rashid so he could pay for the bills when they came. Rizwan used to send me about £300 a month but that soon became £100 or sometimes, only £50. When he first left, he used to call me every day on an old mobile that he had given to me before he left. I didn't know how to call him and I didn't have a number for him but I would press the big green button whenever the phone would make noises. That's what Rizwan had taught me before he left. After a few weeks he would only ring every few days and then eventually it became once a week. The old man stopped coming to the house after 2 months had passed. I was doing ok. I just made sure the children had breakfast, were dressed for school and I would walk them to the gates. Once home, I would clean the house first and then go out and buy the cheapest food I could find to make sure there was something cooked for the children for when they got home. The thought of having a proper family and seeing my mum kept me going.

They boys learnt English quickly and they enjoyed school. It was fun listening to them every evening telling me what they had to eat at the school, what they did and what they learnt. I learnt so much through them. The schools here are so good aren't they? I couldn't believe that they give children food, make them do sports and take them for days out too. The boys really helped me learn things like which foods we could eat, the history of England, the government- they helped me learn so much. They told me about one of the kings England used to have, how this king had 8 wives- I was sure he was Muslim. There were little things that I had to figure out myself, things like putting the bins out for when the trucks came to collect them and remembering the day and which coloured bin needed to go out on which day. I used to copy the rest of the people on the street. Isn't that great? That these trucks come and pick your rubbish up every week? For free! Sometimes at night when the children were sleeping, I would lie awake listening to the drunk people walking past the house. Sometimes they would sing loud songs and I would laugh, other times they would shout at one another and I would get scared. I didn't have any trouble with the *gorey*, no one said anything to me and I just went about my everyday tasks. On the weekends, once the cooking and cleaning was done, we would all sit together and watch TV. Rashid had bought an old TV and a VCR for us. I had lots of old video tapes that I used to watch again and again once the children had gone to bed and the TV was free for me. I used to watch my wedding video quite a lot. I missed my mum and I missed Pakistan. Watching my wedding video was the only way of seeing my mum, sisters and friends. I often sat by myself in that house crying and waiting for the children to finish school. I was so lonely. Rashid and Shanaaz visited a few times, it was good to see them and have some adult company.

Anyway, time went on like this and quite a few months had passed before Rashid told me, during one visit, that I would soon be able to move to the same town he lived in and I would be closer to everyone. The town where Rashid and Shanaaz lived had a lot of Asian families from the same village as me. I was so excited and looked forward to being in a place where there were people that I knew and people that I could talk to. Rashid wrote down a long number for me on a piece of paper that same day and said if I called that number I would be able to speak to my mum. He showed me how to make a call and how to add credit to the mobile. I still don't understand what the *goree* is saying when I ring the number to top up my phone! I just start putting the numbers in like Rashid had shown me and it always works! The first time I heard my mum's voice I just cried. We both did. It had been about 8 months since I had spoken to her and we just cried and cried. I soon shut up though when she said we had to stop crying and talk because the money runs out very quickly on a mobile. After that I would call her every week. She would tell me everything that was happening in the village and all the things that my aunts and uncles had been saying to her. She told me she had fought with Rizwan's mum when she found out that we were not coming back. Mum said that everyone knew I was not going for a holiday, everyone but me, the children and mum. Mum and my mother in law fought again when mum found out that Rizwan had left me in a strange city all alone and gone to America. I loved my mum so much at that point, it felt like she was the only one fighting for me. My mum knew more than I did about *my* situation. She told me that Rizwan and Rashid had hatched a plot to get us, as a family, into the UK using fake bond documents to show we were very wealthy. Once he was in the UK, he was able to fly to America for a holiday and then he disappeared there. Mum told me that Rashid had told the authorities in the UK that I was alone, destitute and it was dangerous for me to go back to Pakistan. By saying all this, I was able to claim asylum for me and my children. The brother's plan was that once I had settled in the UK, Rizwan would come back to the UK as my husband, we would all be allowed to stay in the UK. I couldn't believe that they could do all of this and no one from the government came to speak to me about it. No one asked me if any of that was true, if they had I would have told them that they were all lying! I would have happily gone back to Pakistan to live with my mum if I had known the truth.'

I ask Parveen about her relationship with her husband after the conversations with her mum.

'Well he finally visited me about 16 months after he had left. I remember when he called to tell me he was coming to see us all. We all wore new clothes and even though I was still angry with him, part of me was happy he was coming back. I wore a new *shalwaar kameez* and cleaned the whole house. The children were excited to see their dad and they even helped me to clean up. I cooked all of his favourite dishes and eventually he arrived with Rashid and Shanaaz who had driven to the airport to pick him up. He looked really smart and was wearing a brown suit and tie. He bought toys for the children and these little computers that looked very expensive. He bought me new clothes and some jewellery too. When Rashid and Shanaaz eventually left, we lay together as man and wife. I asked him if he was staying for longer this time. He told me no, he was only here for two weeks and would be leaving. I started to cry and then sob and then shout. I asked him why he was doing this to me? We had been married for nearly 7 years and we had not yet lived as man and wife properly. I told him I felt like I was something he could just use, have children with and then leave. I asked him to kill me, I begged him to kill me and put me out of this miserable life but he just lay silently watching me. He hugged me and told me to stop being silly and that he was doing this for all of us. He told me that everyone has to go through the bad things to get to the good and this was all a test sent by Allah and I needed to remain strong to succeed. He said he was working hard, earning lots of money so when he finally returned to England, we would be able to buy our own house and live as a family. I eventually calmed down and we spent a few days together as a proper family.

Rashid and Shanaaz joined us on a few occasions and we would all go out together, eating, shopping and pretending everything was fine. At the back of my mind though, I knew Rizwan was going to leave me again soon. I asked him at night whilst he lay next to me, what he did in America and what was it like. He told me he worked in a hotel and it was very nice. The weather was nice and there were lots of opportunities to make a lot of money. He said he was close to getting his green card and it wouldn't be long now maybe another year or two. Once he got his green card, he said we could choose if we even wanted to stay in the UK or whether we wanted to move away and live in America. He told me that his manager at his place of work only allowed him a set number of days off per year and so he had to use his holidays wisely and spread them out over a year. If he took them all at once then he would not be able to see me or the children for a year at a time. I was desperate for him to come back and I was desperate for him to not leave me. In those moments when I was completely alone for hours and hours listening to the clock ticking away, I used to think about what would happen to me if he left me. I would be stuck in this strange and cold country, all alone with my children and no one would help me. It used to frighten me, just *thinking* about being all alone used to frighten me. I would end up doing my *wuzu*, praying *namaz* and asking Allah to stop anything like that from ever happening to me. I made so many *du'as* for the health of my children, for the health of my mum and my sisters. The biggest *du'a* I would make was for Rizwan to not leave me. I prayed that my marriage would survive and I would pray for Rizwan's safety and his health. I didn't want a life of loneliness, as a single mum bringing up three children alone in a foreign country.'

She stops and wipes tears from her eyes. Her khol smudges around her eyes, making her amber eyes blaze even brighter, as though on fire. She has beautiful, honey coloured skin, full lips and a nose perfectly proportioned to her face. Her normally glossy black hair is shielded by her duppatta which is wrapped tightly around her head. She wears a loose shalwaar kameez which is the colour of dying mushrooms. A boring brown more suited to an elderly female not a young, beautiful woman like Parveen. She still has a look of innocence about her and her eyes widen in disbelief or narrow in disapproval as I tell her about a recent trip of mine or about something I have read. She has an expressive face-which can be read like one would read a book.

'I found out I was pregnant about 2 months after Rizwan left for America again. The first person I called was my mum, then Rizwan then aunt Rabia and finally Rashid and Shanaaz. They were all happy for me. Rashid and Shanaaz visited a few days later, bringing lots of food and gifts for the children. Shanaaz helped me to make appointments with the doctor and I kept them all as best as I could. My doctor was Asian so I was able to talk to him in my own language which was a great help. Shanaaz would come to some of my appointments with me when she could. When I was 4 months pregnant, Rashid came to visit and tell me that I could now finally, move to the same town as him. He had even found me a small house and a kind landlord who would accept council payments as rent. The children had to change to a new school and Rashid took care of most of these changes. When I arrived in my new home, I was greeted by people I had not seen in a number of years. Both of my uncles - my dad's brothers, were the first to arrive with their wives and their children. They apologised for not coming to see me whilst I was in Birmingham. They did not give me a reason for not visiting or calling. I also met with distant cousins from my village in

Pakistan who were all living in England now. The daughter of one of the women from the village who used to sew clothes for us came to see me. The daughter of the woman who lived three doors from my mum's house in Pakistan came to see me. Some of the people I met I did not even know and my aunt Rabia had to tell me who they were; 'This is the milkman's, wife's, sisters daughter', 'This is the son of Yasmeen, who's sister went to the same school as your youngest sister did in Pakistan.' It felt so good to be part of a community again and be surrounded by people that knew who you were and who would talk to you. The first few weeks in this new place were wonderful. I didn't mind too much if Rizwan only called me once a week because I was often at my aunt Rabia's house or the house of a friend. I had friends, family and companions. They were all good to me because of my uncles who are powerful men within the community. Everyone in the community knows who they are, as soon as their name is mentioned everyone knows straight away who you might be talking about. My uncles are highly respected in the community. People come to them for advice, for money, for favours. It doesn't matter if what they need relates to this country or if it relates to Pakistan, they are so well connected they can help in all kinds of things. I found out later that they were the ones that masterminded me getting to England so Rizwan could carry on to America. I found out that they had done this dishonesty a number of times and for different people. My eldest uncle admitted it himself one night when the men were talking about helping someone in the community.

My uncles love Rizwan and Rashid as though they were their very own sons. They doted on their younger sister and were very protective of her- my mother in law. They were family men and put their own family before anyone else. They have a rank in their families, it's their parents first, then their brothers, then their sisters, then it's the sons and nephews followed by daughters and nieces. After that it's their own wives or wives and husbands of their brothers and sisters. Somewhere right at the bottom are their *bahoo's*- the wives of nephews, the daughters in law. That's why my mum was cast aside as she was when dad died. That's why us sisters were divided up and had to marry our male cousins as my uncles dictated. They only do what is best for the family and what is best for them. They think that they are better than everyone else too, just because they are from a high caste and have lots of money. I never understood it, the men become so proud, so arrogant, people are people aren't they? What is the difference? Don't we all bleed the same? I loved those first few weeks away from Birmingham, everyone was kind and caring. I had help from my aunties and their daughters who looked after my children for me, helped me with cooking and cleaning and gave me companionship. I was invited to my aunt's house most evenings and we would all eat together and then sit and laugh about our times in Pakistan.'

One of the last times I had seen Parveen was when she was in hospital. I remember how shocked I was when I saw her lying in a hospital bed, her eyes glazed over as she lay silently. Two of her aunts were sat in the corner, their eyes puffy and red. They used the shawls covering their heads to wipe away any tears which dropped from their eyes. I ask her about this time of her life.

'I found out through my aunt Rabia. I went to my eldest uncles house one afternoon, like I normally would, and I saw my aunt Rabia had been crying. My uncle was really angry. As soon as I stepped in he started to shout at me, 'Here she is, look at her, these women, they have air between their ears, here she comes all innocent.' I said to him 'Tell me what's wrong, what have I done?' he said, 'Your crazy mum, your prostitute mother, she was always a whore, she is a whore! She has beaten up my sister- *your* husband's mother- your very own mother in law! She has cracked her skull open, I will make sure she gets what is coming to her, and you all can just sit back and watch and do nothing. I will make sure.' My aunt at that point erupted at her husband and shouted at him 'What else could she do? What else can a mother do when she sees what is happening to her daughter?' I knew then that this concerned me but I didn't know anything else. My aunt carried on screaming at my uncle 'All of your life, you put your brothers and sisters first, before everyone, before your children, before me, for Allah's sake do the right thing here. You know this is not right, someone should have at least told Parveen or her mum. How do you think I would feel if you gave permission for something like that to happen to one of our daughters?' He roared back at her 'There is no need for you to know! Know your place in this house! It is to cook and clean not to give me advice or match me in stature. I am the man of this house, do you understand? I am. Not you. What I say goes and that is final. My daughters would not blink an eyelid and would do whatever I tell them to. They are my daughters first!'

I still just stood there listening to them shout at each other. He would shout then she would shout back louder and I, just standing there, had no idea what was going on. I think I remember thinking that my aunt is trying to stand up for me. My aunt carried on 'There you go, you have no respect for me, you have just proved that you don't care about me. You think all women are stupid? That we have dirt and air between our ears? What about your sisters? Both your sisters? Why do you talk to them about family decisions? Why did *they* know? Why did Rizwan's mum know but no one bothered to tell Parveen's mum? Parveen who is the mother of his 3 children? Look at her life- you all shoved and pushed her into a big city to live by herself, she can't speak the language but none of you helped there, you just threw her there like she was a piece of rubbish! You treat your pet dogs in Pakistan better! You let her husband gallivant to any country he wanted and as if that wasn't hell enough for her, she now has to contend with this?' I was scared now and thought something had happened to Rizwan so I started to cry. I stood there, on my feet, 6 months pregnant and just cried. I asked them to tell me what was happening. Why did my mother hurt Rizwan's mother like that? Why was uncle so angry with me? Why was my aunt so angry with her husband? My aunt came over to me and sat me down. She took hold of my hand and said, 'Rizwan has re married in America. He has a *goree* wife and has a child with her.' I instantly said 'No, no you're lying, there has been a misunderstanding, there *must* have been a misunderstanding. Rizwan is married to me, he has 3 children with *me*, he said he is *working* in America. He took oaths on the children's lives.' 'How do you think he got his green card you silly child' my aunt said. 'He married an American.' I started to sob. My uncle who was still stood up watching me and my aunt talk said 'Look my child. Know this and know this well. It will do you good to accept this. In Islam, men can have many wives, you are fortunate that you are his first wife and have borne him 3 sons, you will have the right to his wealth as his first wife. Don't make life difficult for Rizwan, he is working hard to make a life for you and the children.' Well, that was enough for me. It was enough to make me go mad with anger. 'I didn't ask for this life' I screamed at my uncle. 'I didn't ask for any of this. Why are you doing this to me? What sort of life is this? I don't want it. I don't want this kind of life. He is doing nothing for me, everything he does, he does for you and his mother not me!' I have never screamed like that at my uncle before. He turned to my aunt and told her to keep me in line otherwise he would make sure that Rizwan *does* divorce me and with that he walked out of the house slamming all of the doors.

I sat and sobbed with my aunt. She cried with me and said 'We are women, nothing else. Our lives are different to the men's lives. Don't let this destroy you. Be strong like me. I have survived 40 years with him, through the beatings, the insults, the things they did to my family, to my daughters-everything. We have no voice, no reason with men like these. The *goree's* are better than us, they have freedom but we are not *goree's*. We are Pakistani women, this is our *kismet*. You are blessed, at least you can spend your life away from him and away from all the troubles that men bring with them. You are his first wife too and you have three sons by him, all his wealth will come to you when he dies and remember too that you have secured a future for your children in *this* country. It is a better country than Pakistan, so much better. Here, people will care about you and look after you. Care for your children, your boys, they will look after you, I can already tell your boys will look after you so just focus on them now. And look after your own health, remember that baby inside of you.' I stopped crying quite suddenly. I don't know why but I just felt like I did not want to cry anymore. I accepted the offer of tea from my aunt we sat there and made small talk. All I could think of was my mum. I wondered what they had done to her for hurting Rizwan's mum. I asked my aunt if she knew anything about my mum, she said not to worry, no one had harmed mum but she advised me to ring her and tell her not to do anything else. My aunt said to convince my mum that I was happy with the arrangement and to tell mum that I gave Rizwan my blessing to go ahead and have a second wife. Aunt Rabia said this would protect my mum. She said 'I have always admired your mum, she is fierce but sometimes, she says and does things that she should not do. Hitting one of their sisters… these men won't stand for that. She has no one protecting her in Pakistan, they will kill her or stop giving her money and make sure she starves to death. You need to make sure that your mum calms down and doesn't say anything more. I'll help you get your mum to England, then you can be together here, mum and daughter and grandchildren. Does that make you happy?' I smiled but still, all I could think about was whether this was really happening.

I left to go and pick the children up from school but my aunt would not stop calling me. She insisted that we all eat together and so I returned to my uncles in the evening and we all sat there and talked. Rashid was there too and he didn't say a single word to me. Shanaaz stopped me in the kitchen when I was bringing out some more dishes for the men and said she couldn't believe it when she had heard what Rizwan had done. She said that all men are bastards and that she was angry with her husband Rashid for condoning his brother's behaviour. She also said the same thing her mother had said to me earlier. That for women like us, this is the way it is. We had *roti's* with *ghosht* and *sabzi*, there was *dhal* and roast chicken too. The men tucked in, laughing with each other sat at the table. We women sat on the floor eating after the men had finished at the table. I had a small amount to eat even though I wasn't hungry. I felt like I had to eat because they were all watching me really closely. I laughed and joked with them towards the end of the night when Rashid started telling stories from when he was a child in Pakistan. Rashid was always good at telling funny stories so laughing wasn't so hard for me.

I went back to my house and put the children to bed. That night I slept really peacefully. I wasn't awoken once during the night and in the morning, I felt really refreshed, as though I had slept for a number of days. I walked the children to the school gates and then called my aunt and spoke to her. She was going shopping later to buy some meat and asked if I wanted to come along too.

I said I would. I spent the next few days doing everything that I would normally do. No one mentioned Rizwan and his new wife. No one talked to me or asked me how I was feeling. Rizwan's mum was coming to visit her brother's house, aunt Rabia told me one afternoon when we went shopping. Aunt Rabia was dreading it. My mother in law had a lot of control over her brothers and she would normally pull the strings behind the men- that's what my aunt Rabia and my own mum believed. I was scared of seeing her because I didn't know how to react. I didn't want to be nice to her and betray my mum, who still hated her but I didn't want my uncle to shun me or for Rizwan to divorce me either. Divorced women have no place anywhere. My aunt Rabia advised me and said to just be polite and respectful because she was still my mother in law, the mother of my husband and the grandmother of my boys.

I stood there surrounded by my children when she stepped foot into my uncles house. She came over and hugged me, quickly, before moving onto the children whom she kissed and hugged over and over again. She was making such a big show out of how much she claimed to love them and how they all looked like her precious Rizwan. I ignored what she was saying and walked away into the kitchen where I helped Aunt Rabia and Shanaaz to serve food and tea to them all. We stood in the kitchen talking in hushed tones about how much we despised her, and how we had such rotten lives whilst they all sat together eating the food we had cooked and served. We spoke about how badly they had treated us and our families. My aunt Rabia said she had been trying for years to call one of her brothers over to England so he could make a life for himself but my uncle would not allow it. My uncle had said he would report aunt Rabia's brother to the immigration services if she tried to help him. One of aunt Rabia's young nephews managed to get into England without my uncle knowing on a legitimate student visa. Whilst studying he was also working in a shop to pay his accommodation fees. When uncle found out he was in the country *and* he was working, all without uncle's knowledge, he reported him and the authorities eventually deported him. Aunt Rabia said they had argued for days when he did that and she had packed her bags and left him for a few days too. She said she could not understand why he was so against someone coming across from *her* side of the family. It had cost him nothing, not even a penny. Her nephew had never done anything to harm him and just wanted to build a better life for himself. He just wanted a good education so he came here legally to study. Why did he have to report him for working? He was earning a bit of money to pay for his food and accommodation because London is not cheap. What was wrong with that? He just couldn't bear it though, that someone from his wife's side of the family got here. He could not bear it that she might have support in this country and have a member of her own family here. They like to keep you alone, that way they have complete control over you and can keep you in line. Aunt Rabia said that's why the men called over whoever they wanted but would not help a member of their wives families. They were scared that their wives might have some support in this country and they felt threatened by that. My uncle had even helped other male friends call over their wives or sisters or cousins. He helped strangers and people he didn't really know for money but would not help his own wife or her family. Aunt Rabia had even offered him money to help her, uncle took the money but never helped her. He stole his own wife's money, what kind of man does that? She went on to talk about her children and how many fights she had with him about who her children would marry. My aunt has a lot of nephews and so does my uncle. My uncle said there was no way any of his children would marry from her family. They would all marry the children of *his* brothers and sisters. My aunt went on about how they had fought for years and years on this subject. Her eldest daughter, Shanaaz, had married into uncle's side of the family, her second daughter Mumtaz had married my second eldest uncles son and lived in Croydon with him. Her third daughter Sabina had married my youngest uncle's son and lived a few streets away from them. Her fourth daughter, Alisha, had run away 4 years ago and no one had heard from her since. My uncle pronounced her dead. Aunt Rabia and Shanaaz started to cry when Alisha's name was mentioned. She ran away because her dad was taking her to Pakistan for marriage but she didn't want to get married. Both Alisha and aunt Rabia begged uncle to not do this but he wouldn't listen so one night Alisha ran away. Shanaaz says she gets emails from her but doesn't say anymore. My aunt Rabia cried bitterly for Alisha but then also said it was a good lesson she taught her father. 'She taught him a good lesson, you can't try and cage someone, I am glad she ran away, I hope she is living her life as she wants to.' That's what aunt Rabia would say.

Once all the dishes had been cleared away, we served tea and biscuits to them all and sat in the same room as them. They carried on talking to each other, never involving any of us in their conversations. I had been there for about two hours before my uncles and mother in law changed their conversation and started to talk about Pakistan. My mother in law started to cry and took off her *dupatta* exposing her hair. I could see there was a mark on her forehead. She touched it whilst crying and sobbing to her brothers saying that my mum had hurt her so much. They started to have a conversation between them at that point, my uncles, *their* sisters and Rashid. My eldest uncle said how disrespectful it had been of my mum, he called her mad and said it shows how ungrateful the uneducated can be. 'We have been feeding her for years and only because she was married to our brother. We didn't have to show her any kindness but we did because that's what good people like us do. That's what we are. Yet, this is how we are repaid. I tell you, there is more loyalty to be found in dogs.' I sat there listening to them say these things about my mum. I was sat right there, in the same room as them and they carried on as though I did not exist. I kept thinking about my poor old mum sat all alone in Pakistan. They carried on and said they would cut her off from the family and not give her any more money. My mother in law kept glancing my way to see how I was reacting to everything being said. I kept staring at my feet or at the carpet trying not to let any emotion show on my face. I looked at aunt Rabia and Shanaaz, they were both doing the same thing as me. My uncle said to my mother in law that she needed to tell my mum that if her behaviour did not improve, they would cut off her money and let her starve. They said that my mother in law should take that message back to my mum and deliver it in person. He said that my mum needed to be reminded that they had all done her a great deed by allowing Rizwan to marry Parveen. That is was a good deed they had done and mum needed to remember that and be thankful to them all.

I lost my mind. The anger had been boiling away inside and I couldn't contain it any longer. I just repeated 'A good deed? A *good* deed? What good deed?' And that was it. I started to shout at them all. I didn't care anymore. I told them that I would call my mum over with or without their help. I screamed that I would happily divorce their precious Rizwan and they could have a *goree* daughter in law. I said I would like to see how they would keep her in her place. I told them that the children were *my* children and I would make sure none of them ever saw my boys again. I went further and said *I* would support my mum, I would do whatever I could to support her and bring her here. Rashid stood up, walked over to me and slapped me. Hard. Right across my face. My 2 younger sons started to cry. My aunt Rabia and Shanaaz both rushed up and Shanaaz pushed Rashid and shouted at him 'What are you doing, she is pregnant you idiot.' I started to shake and then the anger just rose inside me and I threatened them. I said I would report them to the police, that I wasn't some stupid little girl and knew that Rizwan used false documents to get into the USA and that they had all lied to get us into the UK. That was the limit they were willing to take. My uncles stood up straight away and Rashid pushed Shanaaz and grabbed me by my hair forcing my head back. My mother in law was saying in the background 'See? See? I told you this one had a sharp tongue. Didn't I tell you? She is just like her mother. A snake.' My eldest uncle threatened me and said 'Try it and watch what we do to you. We will cut you into little pieces and feed you to wild dogs'. With that, Rashid pushed me and I fell to the floor quite hard. I quickly got up, holding the sofa for support, I grabbed my children and ran out of the house, sobbing uncontrollably. Behind me I could hear raised voices between the men and the women but no one came after me. Once I arrived at my own house, I put the children to bed and kept saying to them to forget what they had seen but they wouldn't stop crying. My eldest son was still crying up until he fell asleep. Once they were all asleep I went back downstairs and sat on the floor. My stomach had started to hurt from when I fell. I thought through the night. I thought about all the things that had been said to me and been said about my mum. I felt the rage running through me every time I remembered their words, every time I thought of Rizwan, every time I thought of Birmingham and every time I realised that here I was, heavily pregnant with a 4th child to a man who had married a *goree* in America and only came to see me twice a year. My stomach kept on hurting that night and around dawn, I realised I was bleeding. I called aunt Rabia's house and eventually when she answered, I told her I wasn't feeling well and was bleeding. She came with Shanaaz and we went to the hospital. About 12 hours later I had miscarried. I was distraught. I couldn't stop crying, it was like a sign from God that everything between Rizwan and me was now finished. The only people who came to visit me were aunt Rabia, Shanaaz, some women from the community and you. I remember when you came to see me. No one else did. Not my brother in law, not my mother in law not my uncles- nobody. Rizwan did not call me to ask how I was. Shanaaz said the boys were staying with her and were doing fine. She told me not to think too much about what had happened and to forget about it, it was Allah's will and just not meant to be. I asked Shanaaz how Rashid was with my boys and she said he was fine, he played with them and they have been on the phone to Rizwan too. I remember how much it hurt knowing that Rizwan was speaking to Rashid and his children but had no concern for me. His own wife laying in hospital, having miscarried because *his* brother pushed me. I had done everything he had ever wanted me to do, I was silent, obedient and gave him the boys he wanted. I put up with living alone in Birmingham and I did everything he wanted but still, this was how I was being treated. I meant nothing to them, to any one of them. I *am* nothing to them. When I returned home, aunt Rabia made me a cup of tea and made sure I was seated before she told me what everyone had been saying about me. My mother in law and uncles were accusing me of aborting my own child. They had told Rizwan and he had said he would divorce me because of it.'

Her hands rush to cover her face as it crumples. She sobs silently into them, her shoulders heaving with the sobs. She scrunches up the bottom half of her dupatta and buries her face into it, I have to console her. She sobs, her body shakes with raw grief and she gasps for air in between the sobs. I find myself welling up at the utter injustice of it all.

'He gave me *talaaq* over the phone. He said the words three times and it was done. As quick as that I was no longer his wife and there was nothing I could do about it. I just accepted it, what else could I do? He asked me to do the right thing and go back to Pakistan. He said I should leave the children with Rashid and his uncles to look after. He said England was no place for a lone Asian woman with no family and told me that his mum would look to move to England to help with the children. He just wanted my boys and was saying things like they would all give me and mum enough money so we would never have to worry again. He even said that I could re-marry and start a new life! I was so angry at him, I told him to go and die. I wished him death that day and I told him so. I told him that I cursed him and his life and promised him that I would pray he never finds happiness in life. I told him that I wished he, his mum, brother, uncles, aunties all of them would die. I still find that I get very angry when I think of how easy and quick it was for him, as a man, to just say, I give you *talaaq* three times and that's it. I am divorced. I am no longer his wife. I am a divorced, used woman with children. That's it. *Bas.* Just like that. *Bas.* In those words, my whole world changed. Nothing changed for him, he already had a new family set up, he just carried on. Everything changed for me.

My life became quiet. I woke up for my children, lived, breathed and carried on for my children. I just about live off the benefits that I get from the government but every day is hard. Aunt Rabia comes to see me sometimes but I am not allowed in her house. My uncle won't allow it. Shanaaz used to call me every other day but it is rare that I hear from her either now. I was not so upset by that though, I expected it after all, she is married to Rizwan's brother. I am not angry with aunt Rabia or Shanaaz, they did as much as they could in their positions but I am still very angry at my uncles, aunties and at Rizwan. They really have no respect for women, they think we are nothing, just the dirt beneath their feet and they can do whatever they like to us.

I think about my mum quite a lot and try and save up £10 a month to buy phone credit to ring her. She tries to ring me when she can. I told her to sell the wedding gold Rizwan gave me when we were married- they tried to take it back you know? When he divorced me, his mother sent a message to my mum to return the gold but mum said I had it with me in England. Mum has a small stash of money put away now which she uses to buy basics. She has no electricity but she uses fire for night time so is not too bothered. She keeps telling me to remain strong for my children and for the future. Most of the time I get through the pain of the last few years but what kills me is the loneliness. I feel so alone here. I know that if I saved up my benefits for a year, I would have enough money to buy tickets back to Pakistan but if I go there, they will take my children from me. They will get whatever they want there. At least here, the police will protect me, the laws in this country are so much better aren't they? They look after you more in this country, the women are more valued and listened to. Not like Pakistan, if someone with money tells the police that you are mad then the police will believe them and do whatever is being asked of them. If you have money in your pocket in Pakistan then you have the police too. The women have little rights there, it is so much safer here. I just carry on going when I think of the future my sons will have here. Every time they come home from school and tell me about what they learnt, I know I made the right decision. If they were in Pakistan, they would not even be in school right now. It is the right decision. I am here legally now but it is very hard being here and being alone. I know there are groups in community centres but I can't speak English and I don't know how to get the bus to go there. I walk everywhere and thankfully, the town and markets are about 30 minutes away so I can walk there and back. The children help me with the shopping on the weekends and help me to carry the heavy bags. You know what children are like, they always want big bottles of fizzy drinks, and they are very heavy to carry for an hour! It's good exercise though.'

I speak to Parveen about the possibilities or remarrying, she is only 34 years of age.

'Oh god forbid! What are you saying? No no no I could never get remarried, I'm too old now. I could probably find some old, widowed man who would want me to cook and clean for him but I would rather be alone than be another maid to another man. My mum has been hinting about marrying one of my cousins in Pakistan, her sister's son. He is 19 but mum says it would be a good deed to marry him, bring him to the UK and give her sister's family an opportunity. They are so desperate there, so desperate for a better life. My mum's siblings have lots of children who are just waiting around, doing nothing, just waiting for an opportunity to make something of themselves. It is hard for them. To know that you have no future and there is nothing you can do about it- that must be very hard mustn't it? I do sometimes think that to spite my uncles and Rizwan, I should get married again and bring over my cousin! That would show them wouldn't it? I can imagine their faces, they would be so angry! And there would be nothing they could do about it because it would all be legal! Aunt Rabia even asked me about marrying one of *her* nephews to bring him over, she is so desperate, her family are putting a lot of pressure on her to help them-they are very poor. Poor aunt Rabia, she will never see her family again and she won't be able to help her family in any way, not unless uncle dies soon. She did say to me that she will be free once her husband dies. Maybe I *am* lucky that way because I don't have a husband anymore. I have more freedom than all of those women who are like my aunt Rabia and Shanaaz. This should make me happy but it has come at the cost of my honour, and my respect. People never blame the man, they always blame the women. I am blamed in the community for killing my child and forcing my husband to divorce me. Can you believe that? I try and tell myself that at least I am in a good country, a great country- England is good isn't it? I like how green it is. And the *gorey*. Most of them are really nice to me. I like looking at the young Asian girls, they have such different lives and futures to look forward to. I pray for them. I pray for the girls I have never met, I hope none of them have to go through the things that me, aunt Rabia, Shanaaz and my mum have been through. I don't know how the next 50 years of my life will go. I will live for my children and I will live for god. One day, hopefully I will see my village again. I will see my house and my mother again. I miss her so much. My heart hurts when I think of her, all alone, sitting by the fire, thinking about me and my children. My heart hurts when I think of things like that. One day, god willing, one day soon I will see her again.'

4 SHABEENA

'Yes, I am very happy with my life, why are you asking me such a question? Do you think I shouldn't be happy? Why? What have you heard?'

Shabeena has always had a nervous disposition. For as long as I have known her she quickly assumes the worst and then expects it. I have not seen her in a long time and truth be told, I am most excited by meeting her today because I'll finally know the truth about all the rumours I have heard. Rumours such as she starred in a porn movie, she has had 4 abortions, she has had more than 40 sexual partners, she tried to seduce her uncle, she was a crack cocaine user and had sold sex to fund her drug habit all before she turned 21. And that her hair was not real and she has breast implants. Rumors not generally associated with a Muslim Pakistani girl...

'Really? Fake tits? It's just a good, padded Wonderbra. The rest of the stuff is kind of true, just massively exaggerated. I had an abortion. I have slept with 17 men and I begged on the streets of London. I smoked a lot of hash and burnt a lot of cash. I got into a weird situation with my uncle when we were both trashed and an ex has pictures of me naked which the fucker showed some Asian lads. That's probably where the rumours stemmed from and every time they went from one person to another, they grew a little. That's Asian people for you though, always gossiping about someone else's daughters. Just the other day, this fat cow turned up at my mother in laws house just to tell her all about the daughter of another woman who had recently run away from home. Apparently, this girl who had run away was caught in bed with 4 other men. Four! As if! Like, as if the Paki's would let the girl go if they caught her in bed with FOUR men! They would cut her into little pieces! This fat bitch was just adding on her own bits to make the gossip juicier. The truth was probably that the girl ran away with her boyfriend during the night.

I remember at 13, getting into a taxi one evening to go to my friend Iram's house across town. My driver was a skinny, tall white guy who looked like he had smoked crystal meth all of his life. He also talked too much. He told me his name, which I have since forgotten, and basically his life story which was pretty horrible. Like a good passenger, I listened to him, smiled, nodded and sympathized with him. The taxi fare was about £4 so I gave him a fiver and he was very grateful for the extra £1. Iram's family was always very suspicious of me. Unlike Iram, my parents let me wear western clothing, gave me spending money, let me have all different types of friends, let me have sleepovers and let me go out clubbing. Iram's family controlled everything she did. She wasn't even allowed to come to my house, I had to always go to her if I wanted to see her and even then, we had to stay indoors, we were not allowed out. Iram's family really didn't like me visiting much but put up with me because mum had helped the family out with money a few times. Anyway, I was leaning out of Iram's bedroom window, about to light a secret cigarette with her when her older sister burst through the door and shouted that there was a white guy at the door for me. So down I went, a bit confused at who this could be and there, stood at the front door, was the taxi driver. I noted most of Iram's family, including her nosey mum and aunt, were stood a few feet behind me craning their necks to see better and to hear what was being said and so I stepped out and shut the front door behind me. I had simply left my phone in the taxi and he was being a good citizen by returning it to me. I thanked him for his honesty, exchanged a few kind pleasantries and went back into the house. The women were quick to get back to whatever they had been doing and I headed back upstairs to Iram's bedroom to smoke. About 3 hours later I was back at own house. My mum had a face like a slapped arse when I walked in. She took me upstairs, away from my dad, and said to me 'Tell me truth, what happened tonight? What are you involved in now?' I had little idea what she was talking about so after asking her repeatedly to tell me what she meant, she told me that Iram's mum had called out of concern for my wellbeing. She had told my mum that a white skinhead, tall and muscular, complete with facial piercings, and covered in tattoos, had turned up at her doorstep and demanded to speak to me about drug money I owed. I mean, how did they get that from the skinny taxi driver? So you see, the Asians, they love to exaggerate.'

I have always admired Shabeena's strength and straight attitude. She never talks in riddles and tells you things as they are, regardless of whether you want to hear her truth. As refreshing as this can be, it has caused her to fall out with most of her family and cousins who do not wish to hear, amongst other things, about her past sexual experiences or hurts.
Shabeena was born to Pakistani parents in Southern England. Both her parents are educated to degree level and until their divorce, both were high earners. Both parents were born in Pakistan but arrived in the UK as children with their respective families. They had met at university and lived together for many years before getting married. Shabeena remembers her nannies and the times she spent with her older brothers and younger sister but does not remember much about the time she spent with her parents as a child.

'They just did not have the time to spend with us, any of us. I was luckier than Sabina because I was mum's first girl and she took more of her maternity leave when I was born then when Sabina was born. Nannie Carol raised Sabina, not mum and dad. They were both in the sales industry and I think it was quite cut throat. They used to have a few months of earning fortunes and other months of not earning much. Regardless of what they earned, they used to spend a lot of money every month. They had no idea about saving up and I think they found themselves in trouble a few times. That's what mum told me anyway. Dad is such a pretentious twat. Even back then he was spending money on expensive red wine, ports, whiskies and Cuban cigars. Mum was spending on jewellery, indulging in alcohol and eating out with dad and clients. Mum says that because they had months of no money or very little money, they realised they hated the uncertainty of the situation and so decided on a plan of action. They ended up working their absolute bollocks off to try and save as much money as possible. They succeeded in saving quite a lot of money so they used it to invest into cheap properties. They started with terraced houses, picking them up for anything between £9,000 and £20,000. This was the 1970's and 80's, houses were much cheaper then, not like today. They had a plan of sorts for their early retirement and would talk about all the things they could finally do once they retired. Their target was to retire before turning 50. I guess it was a good plan and they were doing well, working towards it. Just a shame that dad couldn't keep his dick in his pants. That's the problem with most men, they think with their dicks. I don't know how many times he cheated on mum in total but she put up with it for years before she finally decided to do something. I am nothing like her, I would never put up with half the stuff she put up with.'

Shabeena's parents had a long, bitter divorce with legal fees escalating past £350,000 alone. She says that her father had managed to get hide of his wealth offshore and her mother knew this but was unable to prove it. I ask Shabeena about this.

'But that's the trouble with women, they can be so stupid. They let their emotions get in the way. Mum needed to be callous, ruthless and calculating, like a bloke, but instead she let her emotions take over and lost so much. See, what she should have done is when she found out about the first affair, she should have started to gather all the information she could get her hands on. She should have started to collect any documents that detailed where the money was hidden and how he was getting away with it. She should have built up all the evidence and then bang! Take him to the cleaners. Instead, she went crazy and looked like a hysterical idiot in court, jabbering and crying about India, Luxembourg and trust funds in the names of countless people. She couldn't prove anything though because this whole offshore stuff is so complex. You know she is mad now? People laugh at her. You must know this anyway, gossip spreads like fire in the Asian community. They all talk about her because she was sectioned after trying to kill herself numerous times. Dad acts like she doesn't exist anymore. None of us exist for him, he sees us all as failures. Especially me, he loathes me.'

Shabeena laughs. She is a striking looking woman. Her black hair extensions drop to her waist. Her breasts look abnormally large in her tight blue sweater and in comparison to her child sized waist and hips. Her 5 inch heels put her height at about 5ft and 4 inches drawing more looks her way from the passing public. She has sharp features with high cheekbones and a small heart shaped mouth. Her small but feline eyes are exaggerated by thick false lashes which are loaded with black mascara and black eyeliner. Her lids are lined with black topliner, flicking at the outer end of the lashes- perfectly symmetrical on both her eyes. She has thin eyebrows that have been expertly drawn on. Her face is heavy with makeup and her long, black, thick hair coupled with her tiny features and petite frame make her look like a living doll. She talks about the house she grew up in.

'I remember how large the house was. One of my childhood friends would come and stay with us during the summer holidays and she would always say that every time she visits, she finds a new room. I remember the dining room the most vividly. It was about 40ft in length and there was a huge marble fireplace at each end. The room was broken in the middle by a dark wood archway - you could have put a wall there and had 2 large living rooms quite comfortably. The carpet was thick, soft and light brown in colour. There were 8 Chesterfield sofas, carefully placed across from one another, down the length of the room. At one end of the room there were mahogany cabinets filled with crystal decanters holding whisky and brandy. Other sections within the cabinet were stacked high with boxes of cigars, statues and watches. The opposite end of the room had a bookcase which had been built into the wall and held hundreds of books. It was magnificent, really luxurious but I never spent more than an hour in that room. It was rarely used by us. It was more of a showroom. Dad's pride and joy. It always smelt of rich wood, leather and occasionally, of stale cigars. We siblings would meet, eat and talk in a small room next to the kitchen. There was a separate room for us to play with our friends in and that came equipped with a TV, a range of movies, magazines, books and some board games. The books were fun, they were on things like periods, the female body, sex and common illnesses. The tiny number of Asian friends that used to come and see us were shocked and horrified. Above the playroom, there was a 'relaxation room' in which there was a music system, a mini bar and a chesterfield sofa which was used as a bed. Dad would often sleep in that room. He had the walls soundproofed so he could listen to music late into the night without disturbing the rest of the house. The upstairs of the house was off limits after 11am. Dad had such an OCD about us getting our grubby fingermarks on his mahogany bannister. On most weekends, mum used to lock us all out of the house at 10.30am with a jug of squash and packets of crisps and then let us back in at 5.00pm. We *had* to play, it wasn't a choice, we *had* to play. We *had* to be out of the house'

I ask Shabeena about her childhood and whether she has many memories of that period of her life.

'I have some fond memories of my childhood but there are not many. I know that we had a very privileged background because we had a lot of wealth. I didn't realise or ever comprehend just how much more we had compared to other Asians until I started hanging around with the local Pakistani boys in the community and saw firsthand, just how poor they were. They used to take the mick out of me for not being able to speak Punjabi, for not understanding Bollywood films and for not understanding the common swear words in their language. Mum and dad spoke English at home and although I heard them speak Urdu and Punjabi to wider members of the family, normally on the telephone, they never spoke to us in *that* language so none of us ever learnt it. The Asian girls at school, and later on in college, didn't like me. They called me a tart, slut and everything else they could think of. They called me a coconut, brown on the outside, white on the inside and to be fair, looking back at those years, I can see why. I was nothing like them. They had to dress in traditional Asian clothing and a few of them wore headscarves. They weren't allowed out in the evenings, weren't allowed to drink or smoke because it was all against their religious beliefs. The whole religion thing was odd for them to grasp too. I identified as being a Muslim but they could not understand why when I ate meat that wasn't *halal*, you know, like the burgers from KFC. And they said I couldn't be a Muslim because I drank alcohol, wore make up, wore tight jeans and smoked. I thought they were just being awkward or looking for excuses to not be my friend. See, dad told me from a young age that being a Muslim wasn't about wearing certain clothes or praying five times a day. He said it was more about being a good person, refraining from eating pork and if you were a woman, to not have premarital sex. Everything else was ok to do. Just don't kill people or eat pigs.

Whenever I think about the whole being raised as Muslim who doesn't eat *halal* food, who drinks alcohol, who doesn't pray 5 times a day, who doesn't read the Quran and who never learnt, I end up thinking that dad just did what he wanted to do in life but didn't have the balls to declare he was an atheist. He still held his sexist and outdated views on women and used the religion, the culture to enforce them. So although we could eat *haram* food and drink alcohol, we couldn't have sex outside of marriage. And although we could go out to clubs and wear what we wanted and spend what we wanted, and even have male friends visiting and staying over, we still had to make sure we didn't cross *that* line. Dad has major issues with his identity and with his status. It must be difficult for him because although he has the money, he doesn't have the status I think he wanted. I think he wanted to be liked and respected in the white community but that wasn't going to happen. To make things worse for him, the few members of the Asian community who used to speak to him soon stopped when they saw Dad eat haram meat and drink himself to stupidity. I think most of his own family like his mum and dad, brothers, sisters etc all stopped talking to him because they are proper Muslims and he wasn't.

I remember him correcting people when they addressed him as Mr, he would say 'No, it's Lord.' I grew up believing that he had been given a Lordship by the Queen for his services to the local economy. He had told us that his services had been recognized by the Queen through all the houses we owned and rented out to local people at a fair price. It was only after speaking to a family friend that I learnt Dad had bought the title from some website. I was embarrassed for him when I learnt of the truth. I felt sorry for him. I guess people treated him differently when he had the title of Lord instead of Mr. I guess it made him feel better about who he was. The thing that always confused me about him is that for an intelligent man, he never understood that to be liked by people, he had to be likeable and nice. He was horrible to some people. So arrogant.

I remember when I introduced him to one of my Bengali friends. He was a boy from a shitty poor neighborhood and was stood chatting with me when dad came to pick me up one evening from a club. Dad didn't get out of his car so I walked over with my friend who I introduced to him. My friend held out his hand to shake dad's hand but dad, he just batted it away like you bat away a fly. I shrieked at dad with a teenage sort of 'Daaaaaaad' screech and asked him what he was doing. Dad just laughed at me and said calmly 'I have no hand sanitizer with me, I am sure this boy will understand.' I was so ashamed and so embarrassed. My poor friend just stood there, awkwardly, looking at his feet. I muttered 'I'm sorry' to him and something like 'I'll call you' before quickly rushing to get into the car. I started to say something to dad about his attitude and how disgusting his behavior was until he told me to watch my mouth and know my place. So I didn't say anything. I just stayed silent for the entire journey home. I could smell the alcohol on his breath and I had experienced his anger first hand when he was pissed. He had a fierce temper, and would become enraged quite quickly and at the smallest of provocation. He used to beat us all when we were younger and I mean beat us senseless. If we were too loud he would hit us, if we were caught upstairs after 11am or the bannister had fingerprints on it, he would hit us. Mum wasn't much better, she would beat us too. They started to hit each other in the later years of their marriage as it was breaking down. It was all so messed up. It's no wonder we all got so messed up.'

Shabeena is estranged from her parents and from her siblings. She is married to a Pakistani man and resides with him and his extended family. She considers them her family and no one else. No one from her family attended her wedding despite her pleas. And even though she begged and pleaded with her father for months to attend the ceremony to give her away, he still refused. He refuses to admit that she is his daughter and has openly told those who listen to him that Shabeena is the daughter of another man.

'I heard about that actually, I even believed it for a day or so. I wanted to believe it so much, to know that I might be someone else's daughter but no, I am definitely his little princess whether he likes it or not. He is a hard man. Growing up, he used to tell us that if we let him down, he would never ever forgive us. He would threaten us by saying that if we ever let him down, he would cut us out of his life and we would be dead for him. I never believed him until he actually did it to me. I was so desperate for him to forgive me, to take me back, to talk to my in laws and to give me away at my wedding. I wanted him to be a wedding guest at the very least if he didn't want to give me away. I had no one from my family attend my wedding. No one turned up. It was just my husband's side of the family present and people still talk about my wedding day because of it. It was embarrassing and it marred my wedding day. I did things I am not proud of but I had my reasons. I was just so angry with him and wanted to hurt him like he had hurt me for years. I wanted to hurt him for all the pain he had caused us all, especially my mum. I wanted to show him that *I* could hurt him. And I did do that, I just never thought of the long term issues that would cause. I never thought of him actually cutting me out of his life like I didn't exist anymore. But he did it, he cut me out, he was true to his word.'

The relationship between father and daughter was always weak but that was tested further as Shabeena grew older and understood more of the interactions between her parents.

'I remember the first time I realised that dad was cheating on mum. I overheard him on his mobile, talking to a woman telling her he did love her and would see her later in the week. Mum was upstairs so I knew it wasn't her. I did nothing, I just registered it. I knew then that the screaming matches and the violence between them was because of the affairs.

Mum's health deteriorated as dad spent more and more time away from the house. I think we had about forty properties by then and dad's job was just managing all the houses and tenants we had. Eventually mum was fired from her job and I'm pretty sure it was alcohol related because by then, she was drinking all the time. I would see her leaving the house whilst tipsy in the mornings so it was only a matter of time. She stayed at home after she lost her job and the arguments became louder and more violent. We had the police come round a few times and dad was taken into custody but instead of letting the police do their job, mum would retract her statement and nothing would happen to him.

I remember the conversation I had with mum, one afternoon in our massive cold lounge when I was 13. I'll never forget that day because quite a lot changed for me. She was slurring her words – that's how drunk she was. She had moments of complete clarity where she would talk sense but then would swing the other way completely and have these violent emotional outbursts. I watched her as she sobbed and then laughed and then sobbed again. She told me about her wedding day and just how little money they had. She made her own wedding dress and there were 3 people present at the wedding. She told me how much she loved him, how he was her world and how hard they worked to built this life together. She said things like 'I sacrificed my youth for him, I gave him everything, I worked and worked and worked, just like him, so we could have a future together, a comfortable and early retirement where we could do everything we wanted to do when we were first in love. Now he hates me. He won't touch me, he won't kiss me, he won't even sit with me or talk to me. Where did I go wrong? What have I done?' I remember consoling her and telling her she was being silly and that of course dad still loved her. She laughed at me and then told me about all the affairs that had taken place. There was one woman, Kate, who he had been seeing for 4 years, the same length of time she had been a tenant of ours. The others were mostly tenants too- married, single, separated, divorced and all were white women. Mum then grabbed my hand and led me, stumbling and falling up the stairs to her room. There was a video on the T.V, on pause, which she restarted and said I must watch it. I sat with her when she played it and saw dad on screen, naked, having sex with Kate in our lounge. It was clear as anything and I still see those damn images in my head. Mum broke down again. She then told me she had confronted him with the tape and he didn't deny it, instead he told her about all the others too and said it was something she needed to get used to if she wanted a life with him. He told her he had grown tired of her body and of her but he would not divorce her because of the wealth, children and his reputation. He didn't care about any of us - just money and possibly his reputation. He only ever wanted to protect his wealth. Mum said she had suspected Kate was coming to the house after a neighbor said something to her and so she set up a video camera, partly hiding it behind a cushion. A surge of hot rage ripped right through my body as I sat watching that tape with my mum. I had started to dislike dad for events earlier anyway but at that very moment, I hated him. Mum was broken. Her makeup was smeared, her eyes puffy and her face swollen, she looked a complete mess. I stayed with her until she sobbed herself into a drunken sleep and then I went out. I met with friends and smoked cannabis for the first time that night. It worked, it mellowed me out and I found myself laughing at nothing with my Bengali and Pakistani friends.

A few weeks later I heard them arguing and instead of staying in my bedroom this time, I went downstairs to hear them better. Mum was threatening him, saying she would kill herself if he did not stop his ways. Dad was telling her to behave and be sensible. He sounded so condescending. She called him a bastard and said he was definitely his father's son, cheating, lying, deceiving and it was no wonder his father wanted nothing to do with him. This hit a nerve with dad and he became nasty. He said to her 'Ok, you want to know why I am doing this? Ok, you are ugly. You are sagging. Your tits are sagging. You have loose skin around your stomach, covered with stretch marks - it makes me feel sick when I look at it and when it is against me, when it slaps against me. Your arse sags, your thighs are covered in cellulite. You are loose, I have had no pleasure from you for years because you are so loose. You smell, you don't wash properly, your body smells. I am tired of you. And Kate is a better fuck than you. I enjoy her body, it's firm and soft and tight. You are a mess.'
At the time, listening to all of this, I remember feeling sorry for my mum at first but then feeling happy when I genuinely thought I could help her. I remember thinking I will get her to join the gym, I'll even join with her! I didn't quite get all of it then. I didn't understand the power he had over her and just how much it damaged her to hear those things. Things she couldn't do much about unless she resorted to extremes and had implants, liposuction, vaginal tightening I mean, what do you do about ageing? Its one rule for him as he becomes more distinguished, powerful and therefore more desirable but mum becomes haggard, saggy and old.

That night was the second time I smoked cannabis with my friends and from then on, every time mum and dad fought or every time I felt angry, I would go out to smoke and get drunk with them. I started to like one of the boys and had my first kiss and drunken fumble with him.

Mum eventually left the house and started divorce proceedings against him. She found herself a small flat she could afford and dad let her take some money out of the joint account. He just let her go and let her exist in this box of a flat. Her mental health went down the pan as she attempted suicide on 3 different occasions. On her third attempt, she sent me a text to tell me she was sorry and that she loved me. I rushed home from school to find her passed out on the dirty floor of her flat with her anti-depressant pills everywhere.

I did not really have the choice of moving out from dad's because there was no space in mums flat. Dad had already told the authorities about her suicide attempts so it was judged safer for us to stay with him. It probably would have been safer at mums because dad was hardly ever home. We cooked for ourselves and looked after each other. My little sister was with our nanny more or less all the time, I hardly saw her. Whenever I could, I was out drinking and smoking.
The first guy I slept with was a Pakistani boy aged 26 - I was 14. In hindsight now I can see it was never a serious relationship for him. I wasn't a serious girlfriend for him, just something he wanted to play with. I probably *was* looking for a dad, a father figure, in some twisted way, someone who would protect me. I became quite wild and started to wear extreme make up, bright colours on my eyes and lips. I would wear the tightest jeans and highest heels I could find. I enjoyed how the girls hated me and how the boys could not stop staring at me. I liked the attention I got from the boys and I liked the power I had over them. It felt nice, being wanted felt nice. This guy, the 26 year old, I'll call him… Mo, he really chased me. He used to take me for long drives in his car and we would spend hours together smoking weed. He was basically a dealer and so always had a stash he was happy to share with me. He was the first guy I slept with and I was really drunk and high when we did it. After that I was obsessed with him. Before we got together, I knew of him because he had been seeing other girls from my school and so I think deep down, I already knew his reputation and what he was like with girls. I think that's why I became obsessive and suspicious of everything he did and said. He stopped lavishing attention, presents and weed on me a few months into the relationship. We would basically get together and have sex, that was it. That was our relationship. He eventually stopped giving me weed for free so I knew then he was probably with another girl. When I eventually found the evidence in the form of texts on his phone, I flipped and I hit him. I actually, physically, beat him up. I was always skinny and small but I can fight. I clawed at his face, punching and kicking him. I managed to draw blood from his face, that's how deeply I managed to scratch him and he still has the scars…apparently. He dumped me, called me a psycho bitch amongst lots of other nasty names so I threatened to report him to the police for rape. I was 14 after all and I wasn't stupid. He always made sure I was completely drunk before he pounced on me

and I didn't really want him to do it but he did it anyway. He called my bluff on it though and said to go ahead and report it to the police, 'Let's see what your dad makes of the whole thing', that's what he said. Of course, I was never going to report it. That one time I wasn't happy but for that one time, there were other times when I didn't mind having sex with him. It was just him laying on top of me pumping away. It's different when you look back now and see things for what they really are. It was rape. I was a child and used to lay there and just let him pound away at me in order for his own sexual gratification. I remember smoking a joint once whilst he pounded away. I was never sober when we had sex. I was always high or completely off my face with drink. If I had my time again I would make sure I reported it but it's different when you're a kid. You don't think like that and there was no one to speak to about it. It wasn't even pleasurable like it is now with my husband. Anyway, I'm a big believer in karma so he will get his comeuppance one day.

I was really bitter after he dumped me and I did go a bit crazy. I self-harmed, I threatened to kill myself, I would call him constantly and leave crying messages on his phone, begging him to take me back. I would get no response from him and so I would leave other messages, some which threatened to report him to the police and others when I was just verbally abusing him. He just did not respond at all to me and eventually I stopped.

I was smoking weed every night and started sniffing cocaine by the time I turned 15. The divorce was still going on in the background. Mum was still in a bad way, stuck in her shitty flat but Dad was absolutely fine. We were called to court to give evidence and all of us said in our statements that dad used to hit mum and hit us. It was the truth after all. Dad went mad at us and said we were not his children and as soon as the divorce was over, we would have to go and live with mum or make our own way. My brother's left- they were 17 was 18. I get the odd email from them now but haven't seen them since they walked out. My youngest sister was sleeping at the nannies now too so it was just me left in that house with dad. I had nowhere to go.

The days started to blur at that point. I would get into school on some days then spend the evenings, off my face on weed, cocaine and alcohol. I started seeing a Bengali boy and slept with him within 3 hours of meeting him. He dumped me a few weeks after. I beat him up too. In fact, I spat at him, bit him, punched him and clawed at his skin when he dumped me. I started going out with the local boys and having one night stands with anyone who was kind to me. The local Asian boys knew about me and they used to all try and get into my knickers at any opportunity. I was past the point of caring though. I slept with anyone. The worst one was a 50 year old taxi driver, in his cab, completely off my face. I am pretty sure that he was the one who got me pregnant but I might be wrong. I wasn't bothering with contraception so it was only a matter of time. I went to a teenage pregnancy clinic and booked in for an abortion. I went to the hospital for my oral tablets alone. The next day I went in for the internal tablet and sat there, by myself, reading the magazines around me, waiting for the remains of whatever was growing in me to come out. I didn't cry. I didn't really feel anything. I was just really numb. They offered me a counselor at some point when they found out my parents were splitting up but I declined the offer. They had to conduct some blood tests on me before the abortion and the results of these on the day were that I also had Chlamydia so they gave me some tablets to take. Again, I felt nothing at hearing this. I do remember sitting there, all by myself, thinking 'I wonder if my parents have absolutely any idea what the last 8 months of my life have been like?' and I remember smiling when I concluded that they probably have no idea at all.

By the time I was 16 I was a walking skeleton. I failed most of my core GCSE's and did not bother attending school to sit the others.
I was still sleeping around with Asian men but put myself on the pill so I didn't have to go through another termination. Mum attempted to kill herself again, this time they found her naked in the garden having taken a variety of pills she found in her flat. She would often turn up at the house and I would find her in the garden with no shoes. She was always asking about dad and I would have to tell her that he wasn't in and probably wouldn't be back that night. Then I would have to watch her break down all over again whilst listening to her cursing dad, Kate and all the female tenants. Dad found packets of cocaine and weed in my room one day and told me to quit the drugs or leave his house. There was no discussion or attempt to try and understand why I was taking drugs or how long I had been taking them. It was a simple, stop them immediately or you are out. And so I left. I left within hours of hearing his instruction and after I saw just how empty he was with me. There was no attempt to find out why I was on drugs, what was going on in my life that warranted the need. Just nothing from him, no love or care, just an instruction, an order. I was nothing but a nuisance to him. My rage and my pride made me leave. I caught a train to Euston station in London and spent the next 3 nights sleeping rough- I only lasted the 3 nights. It was horrible. There were other people sleeping rough but they didn't really bother me much. I had some money and at first, I kept a small amount aside for my trip back but when I found a local dealer, that small amount soon went on cannabis. I didn't eat for the 3 days I was there. I survived on soft drinks, cigarettes and cannabis. I wanted to go home, living on the streets was not for me but I knew that dad wasn't coming for me. He had not called my mobile once to ask where I was. I ended up begging for money and as soon as I had enough, I got a night bus back home. I stunk. I could see the other people on the bus looking at me with utter disgust and sitting away from me. I could smell the stench off my own body yet still, the bus driver hit on me. He was an old white guy and couldn't take his eyes off my tits. I let him grope me when the bus stopped for fuel. In return for letting him touch, grope, squeeze and kiss me, he bought me a sandwich, a chocolate bar and a can of pop.

The house was empty when I finally arrived back. Thinking back to those crazy days, I see now how desperate I was for dad to just make me feel like he loved me. That's all I wanted, for him to say 'Don't go' or to hug me or anything. But I got nothing. Absolutely nothing. I wonder what was going on with him at that moment in time to completely stop caring about his children? When I eventually saw him I told him that I had been sleeping rough in London and that he was an awful father for not even checking up on me. He didn't say much except things like, 'You are becoming hysterical like your mother, you need to calm down' and 'Well I hope you learned your lesson you stupid girl, don't sleep on the streets whilst you have a bed.'

Although dad was barely talking to me, he was talking about me to his family. I got a call from an uncle who found out about my 'running away' through dad. He was dad's younger brother and lived in Dubai. I had a very weak relationship with him having only seen him maybe 3 times in my life- the last time being when I was 12. I think he always felt guilty for the actions of his big brother and so as dad's divorce went on, he took more of an interest in me. He sent me a ticket and I flew out to spend a few weeks with him. My time in Dubai is still a haze of alcohol and cocaine. My uncle was freshly divorced at 36 and I was nothing like the 12 year old girl he had last met. It's a powerful feeling knowing you can control a man by promising him your body. It is such a powerful feeling knowing that you can make a man forget about the things most important to him when sex is on the table. My uncle was living a party lifestyle. The days were for sleeping and the evenings were all about drinking and partying. His advice to me when I first arrived was to just forget about everything that's happening at home and just enjoy myself for the next few weeks. So I did. I partied and drank and slept to then wake and snort and then drink. Everybody was either smoking cannabis or snorting coke, it was everywhere. I slept with a few Arab men out there, one wanted a relationship but I didn't want that.
Sex was strange. I think back to some of the incidents and can't believe that was me. Naked and bent over someone's car in the hot night, completely drunk and once it was over, putting my clothes back on and partying again. The men were animals, all they wanted was sex and as soon as they saw I wasn't going to play hard to get, they stopped being nice and became very business like in their approach- quick sex and then pretend nothing happened as we carried on partying. A few of them just pushed and pulled me into the position they wanted and I just let them. If something was put into my mouth I obliged, if they pulled my hair and forced my mouth to take their dick deeper then I obliged, if they slapped me I didn't wince, I just moaned and they loved it. I asked a few of them to hit me and they obliged. They quite happily choked me, bit me, hit me, slapped me and I started to like how that felt. They called me things like a dirty little slut, a dirty bitch and would ask me to repeat it back to them. I found it funny that words like 'I am a dirty little slut' made them feel good about themselves. I couldn't really care less about the violence or the words they spat out. I liked it. I liked the pain of it all. I think I was punishing myself.

One night my uncle took me to a private party and I bought a new dress for the occasion. It was a very tight white mini dress and I couldn't wear any knickers or a bra with it because you could see the outline. I remember the way my uncle looked at me when I first stepped out, it was pure lust. It was as though it didn't even matter that he was my uncle, he was a man first and lust just took over. I knew something would happen that night between us by the way he kept looking at me. We got very drunk and I had a lot of male attention but it became my mission to tempt my uncle into doing something that was wrong. I wanted to lure him into making the mistake so I could hold that against him. I think I was looking for reasons to hate men and I was succeeding. We ended up snogging at dawn and he groped around under my dress, we got very close to having sex but he stopped himself and just walked away. I didn't care that he managed to walk away, just that he did something wrong. The next morning he pretended nothing had happened and so I too kept quiet knowing full well that his own mind would probably torture him for the rest of his days.

Within a few days of that happening, I was on a plane back home and was greeted at the airport by my dad who said he hoped I would not do anything so stupid as drugs again. He really did not have a clue about anything. When I met with Mum later in the afternoon, she told me that dad was saying he was penniless in court. The truth however was that dad had moved a lot of his property and money into the names of other people. He claimed he never held any property himself and was just someone who managed the houses for other people. He claimed that technically, he had nothing to his name and was struggling to live. I overheard him telling someone on the phone that he had not shaved for 4 days in a bid to look disheveled in court and give the impression he was under massive stress. I told mum this but there was nothing she could do with this information because everyone just thought she was mad. Nearly all of the houses we owned had been sold or given away. Dad told me the houses were never ours to begin with which was a lie but I let him think I believed him. He was money mad and as mum struggled to feed herself on state benefits, he was eating out every night with different women. I decided then I was never going to let him catch me with drugs again, not because I was scared of him but because I did not want to leave the house- not just yet.

I found myself a job a few months before I turned 17 at a local bar and started to enjoy life a little bit more. I still smoked weed and occasionally took cocaine but nowhere near the amounts I used to. I got on well with my colleagues and enjoyed having something to do in the evenings which did not consist of drinking, taking drugs and getting fucked. I would normally get home at about 3 in the morning and would sleep until the afternoon of the following day. I hardly ever saw dad. I visited mum almost every day and would sit and just listen to her. She had days where she did nothing but talk about dad and the good years they had and how kind he was. Then she would have days where she would do nothing but recount the cruel things he had said and done to her. I think the hardest thing for mum to get her head around was how easily he had moved on without her. And how easily it seemed to rest with his conscious that he was squirrelling all of *their* money away, and not giving mum her fair share. She really struggled with that and kept asking herself whether she ever really and truly knew dad. It was horrific to watch her torture herself like this. She wouldn't keep her appointments with the mental health team and eventually she was committed for 2 months and the divorce proceedings were halted. In those 2 months I still visited her at the hospital and sometimes I would bring my little sister along, she was nearly 12 by then. Mum started to get better and was taking her medication every day. She was on everything from anti depressants to calming medication and other tablets for her blood pressure. She was calmer and thinking more clearly.

At work, I had a guy who would come in more or less every night to talk to me called Nasser. Everyone at work knew him as Naz. I eventually agreed to go out on a date with him and he took me to an Italian restaurant. Over the weeks, as I got to know him, I told him bits about dad, mum and the divorce that had been in progress for years. I also got to know a little bit about Naz. He used to have a lot of cash on him and would buy me anything I wanted. Whenever I would ask where he was getting the money from he would laugh and tell me not to worry. He didn't have a job so I always knew he was a bit dodgy. One evening whilst at his house, the police appeared and arrested him on charges of fraudulently obtaining money. He later told me he had been stealing cheques and making them out to cash. He had also been taking credit card details of different people and spending their cash. There were a few of them involved and he had managed to get his hands on over £50,000 this way. He talked me through everything he did and how they did it and got away with it for so long.

It gave me an idea and over the next few days, I rummaged through dads things and got enough information to apply for 3 credit cards in his name with me as an additional cardholder. I was accepted for all of them online and I had a combined credit limit of £25,000. I requested all the statements to be sent to me electronically instead of through the post. Dad was never home when the post arrived so getting hold of the cards and the pins was really easy. The first thing I did was buy mum a small car followed by a set of new furniture for her flat. I was able to withdraw cash on the cards too so everyday, I was withdrawing about £900 and giving most of that to mum until I got to my limit for cash withdrawals. Once I was unable to withdraw any further cash I used the credit to carry on buying things. The minimum payment on the first bill combined was about £700 but I just used the cash withdrawals from each of the cards card to offset the bill. I bought myself a small car and started taking driving lessons. As I neared the £25,000 limit, I applied for another credit card and got it with a limit of £10,000. I always knew dad's credit history was good, he had a lot of cash put away and had just one credit card which he used and paid off each month. Whilst going through dad's documents one day, I came across a folded, crumpled statement from a certain bank showing a deposit of nearly £140,000. Dad was not technology savvy and did all of his banking in person or sometimes, over the telephone. He got monthly statements which he normally shredded every month. I managed to get hold of dad's bank details and logged on to the bank to see if I could set up online banking. I sent off an electronic request to set up online banking and sure enough, a few days later I received instructions in the post followed by a security key. I followed the instructions on the letter and before too long, I had complete access to the account with £140,000 stashed. I could see from his previous statements that there had been no activity on the account for years so concluded that this was what he was declaring to the divorce courts as his lifelong savings. I ordered myself a replacement card and switched to paperless banking. Once a new card and pin arrived, I remember spending about £12,000 in one day. I bought Naz a Rolex watch and for myself, I bought some diamond jewellery, clothes, makeup and perfumes. I kept them all at Naz's house so as to not arouse suspicion. I logged online and transferred £80,000 to my personal account and the rest to my mum who was able to put down a hefty deposit on a house for herself. By the time dad found out in a few months, I had spent £140,000 cash and he was in credit card debt of £40,000. Credit card debt which had, by now, accrued charges, late payments and interest because I hadn't even bothered to make the minimum repayments after the first month.

By the time dad found out I already had most of my things at Naz's house. He said he was going to call the police so I very calmly told him that if he did, I would report his little brother for rape. And I watched him as his world crumbled and he stood there completely powerless to do anything. I told him I had been to a clinic and had the physical evidence that proved my uncle raped me and that all I had to do was pick up the phone to the police. The thing is, I'm not as dumb as my mum. I knew that my uncle was hoarding all the cash that dad really had and if my uncle's freedom was threatened then dad would lose *all* of his money. He couldn't do anything except call my bluff and still report me in which case, my uncle would be arrested and dad would lose his money. It was lose/lose for him and I knew he would keep his mouth shut and just write off what I had taken because the wealth he had hidden away was worth so much more. I heard nothing from my uncle or my dad. Dad offered the family house and a lump sum to mum as a settlement and to stop the legal bills piling up. Mum accepted the offer on my counsel. That was hard work, she wanted much more and it took days to get her to agree to what she was being offered.

Naz and I lived together for about 8 months after I moved out from dad's. My relationship deteriorated with Naz who started to rely on me for money, money which I did not want to share with any man. I eventually left Naz after cheating on him with my now husband. Naz was distraught and sent naked pictures he had of me to his friends which is where the pornography allegations stem from, I think. I broke dad but I got a fair deal for my mum. These men, they can be complete bastards. My husband is a good man, he knows nothing about my past and thinks he was my second lover with Naz being my first. I was able to use the money I transferred to my own account to put down a large deposit on a house, pay for my own wedding and set up my own business. Dad remarried- a woman from India, she is 22 and they live together in another house. I had hoped he would reconcile with me after some time had passed but he never got over the humiliation of being put in such a powerless position. I did feel sad a few years later and I have cried over the death of our relationship. I apologized for the things I did but he didn't want to know.

Mum lives alone and has managed to get another job. She will never marry again and is content with spending the rest of her time on this earth alone, which saddens me. Sabina gets on really well with dad and sees me as a villain which I probably am. But I think as she gets older and sees how the world is and how dad is, she will change. In fact, I have seen a change in her over the past year, she has visited mum on a few occasions and has started asking questions around why they broke up. I'm not going to fill her head with things, she needs to make up her own mind. All I know is that I blame my parents for my lost years. Yes, mum was messed up and looking after her whilst she tried to find new ways to try and kill herself was hard but, dad's demeanor was worse. His attitude towards his wife, *his loyal wife*, his children, his wealth- everything was disgusting. The way we lived together, all under one roof but still as strangers was disgusting. All of his attention was directed towards preserving his own wealth and having a good time. There was nothing for mum or for us. What was truly horrible though was the way he convinced himself that I did everything I did under orders from my mum. He just could not comprehend nor accept that my actions were a result of *his* actions. If he hadn't beaten mum up, had affairs, said cruel things, if he had stopped my brothers from leaving, had been fair to my mum, had been caring with his children then things might have turned out differently. I tried for us to become a family again but we were never a family unit in the first place. I think we just end up wanting what we don't have. I wanted to have an Asian wedding that was done properly, where the dad gives his daughter away and where the parents cry at the sight of their daughter leaving them. Where there is dancing, music, red henna, lots of food and well-wishers. As a young girl, I used to dream of my wedding, the red and gold dress, the jewellery, the sparkles, the laughter and the dancing. I used to see myself as a busy, modern mum with a wonderful husband and a large extended family. I used to imagine my dad as a loving grandfather and my mum as a sane grandmother but it just did not turn out that way. It all went wrong. When I was little I used to think that adults knew everything. That they would never get into trouble or have issues like I did when I was growing up. The truth is so sad. Adults are just as broken, lost and messed up as kids are.'

I wonder if she really is telling me the whole truth. Or whether this is an elaborate revenge fantasy she tells people to make herself feel better. I don't know why I can't shake that feeling off. Mingled with that unease is an overwhelming sadness for Shabeena as I sit listening to her. She has built up a very strong exterior, and no one can get in. The makeup and the hair pieces may all be a protective mechanism to stop people from getting in. She would loathe me for saying this but I find her very vulnerable still. I want to ask her more about her relationships with the men she has encountered and how she really feels about them.

'I don't know why you are pushing on this subject, it's not nice having to admit that I do feel used. And I do feel dirty at times. I was just so messed up and some of the men could see that and they took advantage of it. But I let them take advantage of me. I let them do that.'

She then changes her mind and insists that she was in control of her sexual encounters at all times. She wishes to keep a strong exterior, a woman who is fighting and in control and who would not allow a man to take advantage of her. She would not tolerate such rubbish from men as she keeps telling me. She is not like her mother she keeps insisting. And yet she has so much of her mother in her. The same need to be loved, to be desired, the same strength and dedication to her work, the same need to try and fix things and the same fiery anger. The same ability to project the image to everyone who may be looking that here stands a strong, successful and confident woman. A woman who you will not and cannot mess with. I ask her why she has not been open with her husband about her past.

'He is fantastic, he really is. But he is still a bloke. I don't think it's an Asian man mentality, I think a lot of men would struggle to come to terms with my past and would struggle to accept it for what it is. Actually, it *might* be an Asian mentality thing. I think a modern white guy could come to terms with it, just about, but an Asian guy would really struggle. He struggled when I told him I had slept with Naz! He made me promise never to talk about Naz and to pretend he never existed. I agreed to that, it didn't bother me and in all honesty, it's not something that I want to think about too much anyway. I see *that* part of my life as a chapter that is now closed. Sometimes when we are out and about, shopping or eating out, I do worry about seeing some of men from my past. Sometimes I worry about him finding out but that worry only stays with me for a few moments. I always come around to the same chant in my head - deny deny deny. No one can prove anything can they? And everyone can talk or gossip so I think I stand a good chance of protecting myself and my reputation. It's a strange thing reputation, had I been born a boy then none of this would really matter. I would be able to get on with my life having recovered from my past experiences. People would probably rally around me to help me recover and get back on my feet. But I was born a girl and it's so different for us. We have to pretend to be holy, pure and innocent. No one wants to save a corrupted girl who has been spoiled and so she has to protect and hide her past. It does make me smile though when I think of how eager men are to believe you when you tell them you have only been with one guy I mean, they *want* to believe it. Even after we have slept together and he has seen and felt what I can do, nothing clicks in his head. Maybe women are wired differently. He told me he had only been with 2 girls before me and only slept with them half a dozen times each but I know he is lying. You don't learn what he knows from having sex 6 times! But it doesn't bother me if I don't know the actual truth about his past so why dig up those skeletons? Maybe he is in exactly the same position as me and has the same thoughts I do. Maybe we are both living in the present and don't want to know the truth about our pasts because it would ruin our present. Whatever the reasons, we are happy as we are at the moment.'

5 SAIRA

I was born into a middle class, educated, Indian family in the Midlands. My father is a practising GP and my mother is a pharmacist. I am the only girl in the family with 3 brothers, 1 who is older, the rest are younger. I am a teacher, a mother to a wonderful little boy and I live with my husband, his parents and his 2 younger sisters. I am the kind of woman who if you pass in the street, you won't remember. There is nothing special about me now. I am just another Asian female you will pass, with straight black layered hair, little makeup, well dressed with a big smile. The only attention I get is from a section of the Asian community who believe women should wear headscarves, Asian clothing or a hijab. I only wear Asian clothes when I am at home. I wear western clothing to work, when I am out shopping, when I am eating out and seeing my friends. I don't wear a headscarf and hope I never have to. I have never worn a hijab and hope I never have to.

My husband is my father's nephew. He was born right here in Bradford and works as a salesman. He has the gift of the gab as they say and a cocky manner. He has the arrogance of an Asian male who has money in Bradford and is very protective of both me, and his little boy. His formal education stopped after he was excluded from his college engineering course for possession of cocaine. It was his second month at college. He started working full time in telesales and has worked within the sales industry for the last decade. I could not do the work he does nor do I believe I could be taught it. I believe the best salesmen are born and not made. I know very little of his life before we were married except that he had a lot of white girlfriends. I feel angry at him for having so many white girlfriends, not because I am jealous or because I find them repulsive but because I find his actions and beliefs so reprehensible. He feels his behaviour towards these girls was justified. They were white and thus there to be practised on. He had numerous white girlfriends to whom he promised the world but did not deliver. He went into relationships with these girls yet never had the intention of marrying them. How many white hearts he must have broken because of his actions. How much sadness. Poor white girls, they never stood a chance. All of my friends at university were white. I loved them. I miss them. I feel grateful for the sexual experiences he has had. I feel grateful for the days he must have spent exploring white naked bodies, experimenting with what felt good and what felt better. These experiences of his have made our intimate times explosive. His sexual confidence borders on aggression. He won't stop until I come. I try not to fake orgasms all the time, instead I close my eyes and think of the years gone by, of single beds, wooden desks, sequin bikinis, Sambuca shots, dark fields, moonlight, white heat, black skin, sweat, laughter and hot summer nights.

I went to a 6th form for females and this was the main reason why I didn't have many Asian friends. The vast majority of the pupils were middle class, white, British girls. The Asians from my high school and from the Asian community either flocked abroad for marriage or drudged into the local inner city college once high school ended for them. I became friends with white girls. The few Asian girls who attended my 6th form, saw my white circle of friends and they moved further and further away from me. It was a nice feeling to be accepted by my white friends regardless of my colour, my religion and my ethnicity. I didn't have a particularly religious upbringing like some of the Asian girls and boys I knew. My parents focussed on my education and had already decided that I would not attend the inner city college but instead, I *would* attend the 6th form, I *would* succeed, attend university and I *would* graduate with a first. I do not have anger towards them for pre planning my academic route this way. It gave me a structure and it gave me a focus. I always remember thinking it would make my mum so happy, so proud and so it was worth doing.

My mum started to look tired when I started 6th form. I never took much notice of her life or her daily grind. I never sat back and thought about how things must be for her. Not like I do now, with a son and a married life of my own. I cried with her when she found out about dads first affair. I was enraged alongside her when she found out about his next four affairs too. I never thought too deeply about her when she would take him back nor did I try to understand her reasons, her constraints, her marriage- her prison. She would mutter the explanations to me, almost an attempt to justify her actions to herself. She would say there was no place in the world for on old woman who had walked out on her husband. She would be destined to a lifetime of loneliness and shame. The ill gossip and taunts would not stop with her, they would extend to her mother, and her siblings. They would all be tainted by her decision to walk out on her serial cheat, doctor husband. And what about the children, what would happen to them? And what about the house? And money? And bills? And the shame? And the shame? And the shame?

Thinking back to those turbulent years in which her heart was repeatedly ripped out and smashed into pieces, I now feel her grief. I remember her suicide attempt. I remember finding the empty litre bottles of vodka under her bed. My mum, the head scarf wearing, educated, part time pharmacist. I remember when the fifth affair was revealed, mum threatened to leave him and take us all with her. He told her in a few strong words to go, he would fight her in court for the children and would win. He reminded her she was mentally unbalanced, he would win. He reminded her she would have to work full time for pay the bills *and* look after the children, he would win. He reminded her that no one would want her as a spoiled Asian woman, he would win. He reminded her that she would be shunned by everyone she knew if she walked out, he would win. The court had ruled, his court had ruled. She tried to enter into a plea bargain with him and requested that he marry these women and have a second, third, fourth wife. This would be more tolerable than the affairs and would quash the gossip, the sympathetic looks, the scornful looks, the ridicule of a women who's man indulged elsewhere most nights. He laughed at her suggestion and said the reputational damage to him would be too great. She hit him. She threw her fists at him again and again and she wailed and she cried and she swore and I stood and I watched. And he stood, and he cried and he did not stop her.

Mum's dark eye bags got worse over those few years. She lost weight and I started to notice the deep wrinkles settling in around her eyes. I saw the grey streaks appear in her normally black hair. I saw the obedience, the loyalty still in her and watched her take care of dad's every whim. Mum kept me sheltered from a lot of things. I would come home from my 6th form and find things smashed around the house, my older brother sat with a cut lip, a swollen eye, brimming with rage, my mum's eyes puffy, her face red and swollen, my dad nowhere to be seen. I often came across this scene of destruction. One Sunday I heard a commotion downstairs. I ran down and saw my mum holding my older brother back. My older brother who was gnarling at dad. My dad's eyes were bulging with rage and he was screaming. They were all screaming and shouting. All this rage pouring out of their mouths. Then my mum pushed my brother, her son. She pushed him and told him to get out. To get out and never ever come back. Her shouts turned into plea's, her plea's turned to begs. She sobbed and begged him to leave and never return. He was crying. Dad was stood there, fists clenched, jaw clenched, eyes bulging and red. I was shaking, quietly sobbing, stood by the doorway watching this scene unfold right in front of me. My brother turned to my mum and said if he left now, he would never return again. He said it a second time, slower, 'If I leave now, if you ask me to leave now I promise you mum, I will never come back. I won't come back.' She sobbed into her hands and whispered to him to go. My brother, the warrior, his head held high, his tears streaming down his cheeks walked towards me. He put his arms around my shoulders and hugged me. He kissed my forehead, looked me in the eye and said 'Look after her.' I never saw him again. Mum and dad were different after my brother left. Dad was a little more loving towards her. They would sit together, they would laugh together and they would eat together.

I think the affairs stopped but I'm not sure why. Sometimes though, when I came home earlier than usual, I would see mum's red face and puffy eyes.

My dad is a boisterous man. He enjoys showing off his latest acquirement, his latest material possession which to him is evidence that he is better than others. When he bought his first Mercedes, he sent pictures of it, via e mail, from our new computer to everyone in his contacts list letting them know he was emailing them from his new computer. He would call people and tell them he was calling from his new iPhone or his new Blackberry handset. He bought me an Armani watch when I started the 6th form. He would tell everyone his daughter was in a 6th form grammar school filled with white, rich people. I smile when I think of his ways. He would make me take the Armani watch off every night and carefully put it back into its display box. When I scratched part of the watch one day, he made the decision that it would only ever come out of its box when there was an occasion, special enough for its use. How he clung to material things and how he felt validated by them. He was now someone who was important, wealthy and successful. This man, who had arrived from India via an arranged marriage to mum had, in his mind, made a successful transition into the western way of life.

Years later when I spoke to mum about dad's job as a local GP, she told me that he struggled with his British educated colleagues who were better than him. They would often have to explain things to my dad, details about new medication, the trials behind them and why they should or should not prescribe. It must have been hard for him, to be in that arena everyday and know that he is not the king, that the others are the kings there. He is only the king of his home and a king in the Asian community. Perhaps that's why he treated mum so badly, because he had to feel manly again. I find it amusing that he never struggled to differentiate between his moral, religious and cultural beliefs. His religious and cultural beliefs tended to come first. He didn't believe in demonic possession or things of such nature but he did believe that women should act a certain way and be a certain way, particularly Asian women. Dad had the occasional stupid Asian girl who would go to see him and request emergency contraception. The community would always find out. If it wasn't dad telling people, it was the Asian receptionist who took delight in reading through patient records or the Asian girls in the pharmacy who took delight when handing out contraceptive medication to known single girls. Thankfully, the instances in which Asian girls saw dad were rare- they would eventually, always see a white doctor. It was well known that a white doctor would take doctor patient confidentiality much more seriously. Some Asian girls would take their prescriptions to other pharmacies having seen a white doctor whilst others just changed their GP practise completely.

Dad treated me well, I was his little girl, I still am, now. I was spoilt by him. I never felt like I had the constraints upon me that other Asian girls had. I was allowed to go shopping with friends on the weekend, I was allowed to have friends over and was allowed sleepovers. I even had a birthday party thrown for most years, which was a grand occasion. Dad would spend days organising the event, sending out invitations and organising the food that would be served. He would always give me my present, a bundle of crisp £20 notes, in front of everybody and just before I would cut my cake. He would make me count it, quite often there would be hundreds of pounds and I would exclaim with joy- he loved that. Some of the women from the community would gasp '£500, *hai Allah*, he is so generous'. After the party finished and once the last guests had left, I would always return the bundle of notes to dad for 'safekeeping' as he would say. Anytime I needed money I would ask him and he wouldn't hesitate. Of course I only ever asked him for £10 or £20, I never needed anymore.

I think mum did fall in love with Dad when she met him for the first time in India. She said dad would tell her he had never seen anything as beautiful as her. Dad's family bestowed many gifts on mum, they were very generous. Once dad arrived into England, it didn't take him long to find a job and his English just got better and better. He never lost that Indian sound though- he could talk eloquently but as soon as he opened his mouth, you knew he wasn't born here. Dad used to be such a proud man, he would act as though he was better than everyone else around him. I guess compared to most other Asian men in the area, he was better because he had a good job, an educated wife, money and status. Mum and dad are much closer now, they are both so loving towards me and my family now. That nauseating pride that once emanated from dad is no longer there. I guess I taught my dad humility.

My friends at sixth form wanted to go onto become teachers like I did but for every one of us, there were many who had no clue about what they wanted to do. I guess I was one of the lucky ones who knew what I wanted to do with my life. Dad was proud of me for agreeing with him and pursuing a career in education- it was such a good, solid, middle class career to have. He would often joke about it and say that I would teach the idiots, he would diagnose their problems and mum would hand over the tablets. My friends from the 6th form would hit the local town on a Friday and Saturday night and although for the first year I didn't join them, I made sure I went out at least once a month with them during my second and final year. I would tell my parents that I was staying over at a friend's house to revise when in reality we would go out.

Some of my friends' parents were extremely understanding. They realised I would be in great trouble if my parents found out that I was dancing and drinking and so when dad would call, and he often did, they would cover for me and say 'The girls are all revising' or 'The girls have just gone to the Indian takeaway'. I was never caught. I kissed my first boy when I was 17, drunk, and had just been sick in the toilets. He was white, spotty with dark hair, bad teeth and was licking a lot of my face. By the time 6th form was ending I had been through three relationships, each lasting no more than a fortnight, kissed about 30 boys and 6 girls. I look back at those days with great fondness. I loved my life then. I felt so free. I *was* so carefree. I laughed and cried with my friends. I danced until dawn with my friends. I walked back with my friends as the sun was breaking, to their homes, barefoot, drinking the milk we had bartered from the milkman doing his early rounds. I flew through my exams as did most of my friends and four of us were accepted onto a teacher training course- we would emerge as teachers after our 4 years. Moving away to live on a university campus was unbelievably exciting. I only felt sad for my mum now that my brother had gone, she was all alone. I would tell myself to not worry too much after all, at the very least, her relationship with dad seemed much better.

University completely freed me. I have never felt as alive as I did during the years I spent there. The drinking and dancing and singing and shouting and laughing and learning. The way you start to think differently, the new things you learn, the independence you experience. I wish my mum could have experienced this side of life. I had that thought about my mum a number of times during my first few weeks. I met Daniel four months into my first year of university. He was Afro-Caribbean with beautiful, dark, smooth skin and bright brown eyes. Shy eyes encased in thick lashes, full soft lips which hid perfect, straight, white teeth. He would walk with his shoulders slouched, his eyes fixed to the floor and had a small group of friends. He was really shy. We had noticed each other on campus and in the dining hall but neither of us had the courage, whilst sober, to be bold enough to walk over and start a conversation. So during one student night out, whilst full of vodka, wine and Sambuca, I saw him looking straight at me from the other end of our student bar and I made my way through the hoards of people until I found him. I took his hand and led him to the dance floor where in a drunken blur, I threw my arms around his neck and put my head on his chest whilst trying to move in tune with the blaring beats on the sound system. Alcohol gave me courage and complete confidence. I was unbelievably sick that night. He held my hair back and handed me tissues to wipe my mouth. In between the bouts of vomiting, he let me rest my head on his chest and kissed my forehead. He spent the night in my room, sleeping fully clothed, next to my fully clothed body, on my single bed. In the morning we were a couple, just like that. Our friends were so happy for us. I was Daniels first proper girlfriend and he was my first proper boyfriend. We fell in love hard and quick. It was such a tremendously odd feeling, being in love with someone. Being so utterly in love with someone. There were times where I just wanted to bite him and hurt him-physically hurt him, I loved him so much. He would spend hours running his fingers across my skin, along my arms, my neck, my face, my legs, my back. He would wrap his arms around me and take huge gulps of air, smelling me, inhaling me. He said he loved my smell. We were inseparable and started to live in each others rooms exploring our minds and our bodies. He was so intelligent, we would spend hours discussing slavery and discrimination. He opened my eyes and opened my mind to so many new things. He forever changed the way I think. He would challenge my views, views instilled in me from my culture. He challenged the role of the female in the household and challenged the religious beliefs my family held. He would challenge some of the beliefs that I held. I used to tell him that I could only marry him if he was a Muslim, otherwise my parents would not accept him or us. He would challenge that. I made it clear to him that this wasn't something that I cared about, he could do as he wanted as far as I was concerned but if he really wanted to be a part of my family and if he really wanted my parents and cousins to fully accept him then he would have to convert to Islam. He asked me what would happen when university finished, would we finish too? I promised him no, this would not happen. I would not allow that to happen. I promised him I would fight for us and my parents, regardless of their beliefs, would accept him and love him if he converted. I told him it was only a small ceremony and he had to utter a few words. Once it was done, we would leave for our own home, we could eat and drink and do as we wanted. We could be the people we wanted to be. It was just a front for my parents and the community to accept him. I said to try and see it as a tick box exercise and nothing more. I promised him that I would talk to my parents about us once university was over, there was no point in causing trouble now, not when we had what seemed like eternity stretched out ahead of us. I guess I hoped that somehow things would work themselves out.

Daniel had our life mapped out for us. We would both buy a house, live together and work as teachers. We would have children- 3 of them, and would live happily for the rest of our days knowing that we were together. I loved listening to him talk about our future. I would close my eyes and I could *almost* see the children, and the house, I could *almost* feel the sunshine on my skin whilst standing in our green back garden, I could *almost* hear the laughter from the children and from Daniel as they played and tumbled together across the green grass. I gave him my virginity and he gave me his. Sex became better as

100

the weeks and months went by and as our love and trust grew in one another. We would have the most open discussions about sex and what felt good, what the sensations were akin to, what would feel better and what would feel even better. We would explore each other, on a single bed, in a tiny room, on a university campus. His dark skin shining with moisture, our limbs interlocked, our panting, smiling, our pain and our pleasure, the taste of his salty skin and the touch of his hands. We had sex wherever we could, our rooms, the showers, the corridors when empty, outside on the grass during summer nights. I couldn't keep my hands or my mind off him. I yearned for him when he was away for a day or two, visiting his mum. I would ache for him, for his smile, his smell, his hands, his embrace and his taste. He would bite me, pull my hair, tease me and make me beg. I would always get him back though and would scratch his back to urge him on, bite him in lust and pull his hair whilst in the throes of utter raw passion.

I remember one summers night when a group of us left campus with tents, picnics and alcohol. We had decided to go camping and make the most of the warm nights. The girls and I sat around in tiny shorts and sequin bikini tops taking in the sun's rays whilst the boys cooked something to eat on the fire and made sure the beverages were cool. We sang songs by the fire, we roasted marshmallows with little success. We toasted to everything that was good in our lives. We toasted one another, we toasted love, we toasted good sex, we even toasted a good block of cheese and a big bar of chocolate. I lay next to Daniel, resting my head occasionally on his chest. He had his arms wrapped around me and would kiss my head, my neck, my lips- any part of me he could. We were all in relationships and occasionally a couple would leave to have sex under the guise of a walk. Daniel and I decided to go for a walk once the moon was out. I remember the night so clearly, I don't think I have ever seen a more brighter moon or the earth lit up as vibrantly as it was that night. The air was warm and gentle and I don't believe I have ever felt as happy as I did on that moonlit night in a field, all of my senses being consumed by Daniel. My body felt like it was ablaze and we were so perfect together, our rhythm, our heartbeats, our breathing. I could feel the blood rushing around my head and in the deepest parts of me, filling me with total joy. I didn't want to let him go that night. I wanted to stay sat in his lap, with him inside of me. I wanted to keep my arms wrapped tightly around his neck and I wanted him to keep his arms around my waist, his breath on my neck. I felt so lucky to have met my soul mate so early on in life. Some people go through life and never experience the joys I had already experienced at 20 years of age.

Mum and dad would visit me every few weeks and when they did, Daniel and my friends would all come together to help me change my room. I had to take down all the photos of me in bikinis, me with my friends, with Daniel, with alcohol, the posters about sex and love. I had to hide away all of my university clothing, the shorts, the miniskirts, the G-strings and sexy lingerie I had, the contraception, the lubricant, the massage oils, the letters and notes Daniel would send me or leave for me- anything that was Daniels. It used to be quite an arduous task at first but we soon got the hang of it. I believe if my parents had shown up on campus in a surprise visit, I would have managed to get my room changed in 5 minutes. They seemed happy with my progress and would sometimes give me unwanted advice on making sure I wasn't tempted by drink or clubs.

For one of our anniversaries, Daniel and I went to the Lake District for 3 nights. We spent the days walking amidst the beautiful landscape, eating in quaint tearooms, laughing and making plans for the future and at night, we feasted on each other. We went to Blackpool one evening with friends and walked around the pier eating chips, trying to win at bingo, eating candy floss and then having our pictures taken in a silly booth. Daniel took me to London another weekend where we watched The Lion King and then shopped, talked, laughed and ate. We walked, hand in hand, amongst all the other different nationalities and colours on the streets of London and I felt at home. I felt we would be ok in London and would be accepted. Whilst sitting in a small café, drinking a hot chocolate with cream and marshmallows, we agreed that after university, we would both look for teaching roles in London and begin our lives together in the big city.

I had met Daniels mum on a number of occasions and we got on very well. She was a strong, intelligent woman who had raised Daniel and his 3 siblings by herself. She adored me and was sympathetic to my issue with my culture, my religion and my parents. She would urge me to speak with my parents and tell them about Daniel sooner rather than later but I told her that I knew my parents, and the way to do this would be once university is coming to an end and they were able to see that I was going to move to London and start a life with Daniel anyway. During one of our hundreds of conversations, Daniel had finally agreed to convert to Islam in order to marry me and although his mum initially wasn't pleased, she soon understood and stood by her son and his decision. For me, a great weight had been lifted. I knew that now he was prepared to become a Muslim, my parents would not mind too much- he wasn't Indian but at least he was a Muslim.

We visited so many cities, so many places together. I secured a job at the local pub where I was popular amongst the locals, most of whom knew about my love predicament. Often people would tell me to run away with him and not care about my parents but all I could think of in those times was my mum, and her eyes. I told my parents I had secured work at the local supermarket and so could not come home during half term breaks or Easter or Christmas. I spent my Christmases with Daniels family. It was just wonderful. I didn't bother with *halal* food, I ate sausages, turkey, beef, chicken anything except black pudding- I couldn't get past the congealed pigs blood. I had so many gifts from his family and from Daniel to open and I found myself really getting into the spirit of Christmas. I spent time with my friends too, one of who would occasionally get really upset at my predicament and my parents. We would spend long, upsetting hours, talking about me leaving my family and starting anew in London. My friends would pledge their support, their loyalty and promise me that they would help me if I needed them. I loved them so much, they were like the sisters I never had.

For our second anniversary Daniel gave me a beautiful ring with a turquoise stone. His mother had given it to him to gift to me when he chose to do so. It was really beautiful- simple and elegant, a thin band of gold with a gold clasp in the centre, within which sat a small round turquoise stone. It looked fragile but it was so beautiful and elegant. I turned 21 and Daniel bought me a silver necklace with a single heart. My dad bought me a car and gave me the keys just before I cut my cake and in front of all of the guests who had been invited to my party. I squealed with excitement. Dad was so pleased with my reaction. It was a lovely red Peugeot 107- 3 years old and in great condition. I couldn't wait to get it back onto campus and show Daniel. We would be able to plan weekends away now without having to rely on public transport- we could drive to Scotland like we had talked about or drive to a port to take a ferry across to France or Ireland.

Our second year finished and we were all due to start our placement year. We would be placed in a school and would have to work as trainee teachers, passing numerous observations and assessments in order to become fully qualified. I went home for the last few days of our Summer break in August before University started again in September. I hated leaving Daniel but I had not been home in months and so decided to spend 2 nights with my parents. Mum looked thinner than the last time I had seen her and older. Dad hadn't changed much. They spoke to me about my placement and where I might be working- I said it was likely to be Manchester and they seemed pleased with that. Dad then spoke to me about getting married. His sister in India had a son who had just qualified as a doctor, he felt this to be a good match. I declined instantly and they were both surprised. When I look back, I think this is the moment that I knew just how much I had changed. I didn't understand why they were so surprised at my instant refusal. Now I realise it was because I had never refused them before. I had always done as they had asked of me without complaint or question. I said I was tired and did not wish to discuss this any further and went to bed. The following day, I went shopping with my mum who was unusually quiet and would study me whenever we sat somewhere to have lunch or coffee. Mum asked me if I knew and realised that I would have to get married one day and I said yes, I knew that but, I wanted to marry of my own choosing. Mum said that was ok and my father would probably come round to that as long as the boy was Muslim. She continued to study me. I wouldn't lift my gaze from my coffee cup. She asked me if there was someone I had already met and I found my head nodding. She asked if he was a Muslim and I nodded again. We didn't talk about it anymore.

Later that evening, mum came to my room and asked me to come and sit downstairs with her and my dad to talk about this boy. I sat downstairs in our living room on a single leather sofa whilst my parents sat directly across from me, next to one another on the triple seated leather sofa. Dad had been so proud when he had bought the leather sofas complete with a recliner chair. He had even invited some of our neighbours and cousins to come and sit on the sofa and sample the soft leather. I never liked the sofa's, the leather was too cold and never seemed welcoming. Mum was looking at the ground whilst dad was looking straight at me. I matched his gaze, but inside I was terrified. He was sitting, leaning forward with his hands clasped, his fingers interlocking together and loosely resting on his lap. I don't quite remember how the conversation started or when mum got involved. I just remember the screaming when I told them he was black and would convert for me. I remember shouting at them both and calling them racists and hypocrites, what did it matter that he was black, he would be a Muslim and surely that's all that should matter. But no. Dad was a different person, he was animated, furious and his face contorted into angry formations that I had never witnessed before. He kept repeating how I had picked a nigger, the lowest of the low, a nigger, a black nigger, what would our children be? Little monkeys? Little dirty niggers? Mum was shaking, crying asking me how I could even suggest something so absurd- marrying a black man? The conversation continued like this. I screamed at them, trying to get them to see just how shockingly racist they were, how wrong they were, what did the colour of skin matter? And they just ignored me and talked about the community, they would never live it down, no one would ever let them live it down, how it was unheard of, an Indian high caste girl, the daughter of a doctor and a pharmacist marrying a nigger. The biggest emotion that captured my entire body that evening was shock. Raw, nauseating, unbearable shock. Nothing made sense anymore. They had said too much, they had told me the truth about their core beliefs and values and even if by some miracle, Daniel and I were to build a life together and have children and they came to accept that one day and came to accept us one day, the words they had uttered today would still stand. *I* would always know that they said these poisonous things. *I* would always know. The shouting and crying continued for a few hours, I did not budge from my stance- I wanted to marry Daniel and they would have to come to terms with his skin colour. Mum held dad as he has sobbed into her chest, like a child. He kept saying 'Where have I gone wrong? I did everything for her, I gave her freedom and nice things, where did I go wrong?' Mum held him and cried too saying 'Maybe we gave her too much freedom.'

I felt an overwhelming sadness that night. Seeing my parents as 2 broken people, imprisoned by their culture and confused by their religion, sobbing at the prospect of losing their daughter. I saw Daniels face appear and disappear, I saw the moonlight on the ground, I saw the lake district tearoom, I saw his smile, I saw my friends lying in the sun, the pub I served drinks in, the face of a lecturer, the purple haze from a nightclub- all appear and disappear. I left the room, I left them sobbing and went to my room and sat on my bed. I sent a text message to Daniel and told him what had happened. He called me and I told him everything they had said. I wept as I repeated the things they had said about him. Daniel told me to get my things and return to campus immediately and I told him that I don't think I could do that. I didn't think they would just let me leave. Three hours later, at around midnight, Daniel was at my parent's door with 3 of my friends. Daniel had awoken Emma, who had a car, told her what had happened and she drove with her boyfriend Matthew, my other great friend Hayley and Daniel to my parent's house. Emma and Hayley were in their pyjamas, stood in our living room, defiant and wonderful and strong. They stood either side of Daniel and once I entered the room, they rushed around me, hugging me and asking if I was ok. I went straight into Daniels arms and my mum gasped and started to cry again. Dad stood and stared at us all. He stared straight at Daniel who matched his gaze unflinchingly. There we were, a group of 5 friends, 1 black, 1 brown, 3 white, 2 in pyjamas, 1 who looked angry and 1 ready for a fight. Hayley asked me where my things were and a few minutes later, Hayley and Matthew had bought my packed case downstairs. I said to both of my parents that I did not want to do this, I wanted to be with them but they had to accept my choice- my choice was Daniel. Dad said I was dead to him and to fuck off. He had never sworn at me before. He told me to leave the car keys, I didn't deserve the car anymore. I decided not to argue and threw the keys on the floor. We all left together, squashed in a tiny Renault Clio. I cried all the way back to campus. The following day I told a trusted lecturer my story. He alerted security and administration advising them to be on the lookout should my parents come to take me home. The phone calls started that evening. At first it was my aunt, my dad's sister, we had always been so close. She sympathised with me and Daniel but said there would be no chance of marriage and acceptance within the community. That I should think long and hard. Would Daniel really become a practising Muslim? What about when we had children, would he object to our 12 year old daughter showing her legs or would he allow it? Or going to discos? Or having boyfriends? Or having sex? Would I? Would he object to our daughter having sexual encounters with different men, kissing boys in parks at 13 and 14? Would he object if I wanted to send our children to a mosque? To celebrate Eid? To fast during Ramadan? Would I object? I didn't want to think about these things. I felt sick at the thought of my daughter having sex with different men. I felt sick at the thought of my children not knowing about Eid, Ramadan, henna, Bollywood films that made me and mum laugh and cry, Bollywood dance routines, Asian weddings and the strange, hilarious and sad customs they came with. I felt sad that I would not have the red and gold wedding that I had dreamed about, the ceremonies, the food, the dancing, the singing, the whole community coming out to celebrate my special day with me. The *doli* ceremony where I would be led out of the wedding hall by mum and dad, both of whom would be sobbing, all the women would be crying, they would take me to my husband who would be waiting, near the hire car, with his family. They would hand me over to my new family and tell them that I am now their wealth. I had a strange feeling of utter despair. I did not want my parents' customs and traditions to die, they were *my* customs and traditions too. I did not feel comfortable at some of their beliefs but overall, I could not become something which I was not. I am an Indian Muslim girl, born to Indian Muslim parents.

Even though I wanted to be with Daniel more than anything else in the world, I would find myself feeling scared or overwhelmed at the prospect of a lonely life. In these situations, I did my *wu'zu* and I prayed to God to help us, to help me do the right thing. I felt uncomfortable and sometimes passed judgement on girls who had a lot of sexual partners before marriage. I know this makes me hypocritical but I found I was able to live with my own relationship with Daniel because he was the guy I was going to marry, he was a serious relationship not a one night stand or a fling. Still, I couldn't shake the guilt that comes with knowing you broke the hearts of the very people who raised you.

We moved away from campus and into a house with some of our friends. Our days were filled with revision and writing our essays ready to see out another year of university and the start of a placement somewhere far away. We had been living together for about three weeks when I really started to miss my family. I spent the first few weeks floating on a wave of defiance- I had broken free and was now with my Daniel. I had done the right thing and broken away from the racist, uneducated, hateful, and oppressive people that were my parents. When I started to come down from the defiance though, the loneliness floored me. I would go to the pub with Daniel and my group of friends and we would sit there, drinking ourselves stupid. We laughed, joked, cried and stumbled home through dark fields, occasionally stopping to empty the contents of our stomachs. It all seemed so empty. I would sit on those padded benches, in that lonesome pub, my drink sat on a weary coaster, my friends sat around me as we talked about the latest celebrity mishap, the latest scandal on campus, or the stress individuals were under with work. And I would find my mind would drift away to thoughts of my mum. I would wonder what she would be doing at that very moment. Would she be cooking and eating with dad? Would she be out with someone? Would she be sitting in my room with my clothes in her hands crying? The conversations shooting off around me suddenly felt pointless. I felt alien to the people around me. They would never experience what I was feeling because they were so far removed from it. They would never be able to understand that I, sitting there thinking of the struggles my father had to face when he came to this country, felt guilty. How could I ever expect any of them to understand it though? Theirs was a different world to mine. *This* wasn't happiness. Happiness was being surrounded by your family who loved you. Yes, they were blinded by ignorance but that's all they ever knew. No one empowered them to stand up against the masses and go against the tradition they and their ancestors were born into. I thought about the times when dad did take on the traditions and culture of the British, they never completely accepted him. To them, he was still a doctor qualified in India, he wasn't as good as an English doctor. He could wear the blazers, type on the latest gadget and smoke cigars but he would never be completely accepted by them. What does someone do in this situation? Leave one oppressive culture behind to try and join one that doesn't really want you?

I struggled living with Daniel. There was nothing he could do to make me feel less guilty. If anything, telling me I was stupid to feel guilty made me feel more and more distant from him. He didn't understand me or what I was going through but how could he? When he left to spend the weekend with his mum, I would sit all alone, watching TV or reading a book. I got a glimpse of what the rest of my life looked like. Yes, people are lovely and my friends invited me to their homes, Daniel invited me to spend time with him and his mum, his mum even said she would be a mother to me too. But it's not the same. She is not *my* mother. You still feel this ache in the deepest part of your soul when you see the joy on a mothers face as she hugs her child. I saw that time and time again with Daniel and his mum. The hugs and kisses would find me too but I could never quite ignore the sympathy these hugs and kisses came with. Not having the unconditional love that comes with parents was hard to bear. Daniels love was conditional after all, he could leave me for someone else and that would be it. Parents love you no matter what. I'd had that shield of protective love ripped away from me and I felt vulnerable, naked and alone. I missed my family, my cousins, my aunts, my uncles, my grandparents- everyone. I felt like small pieces of me were dying with each day that slipped by. My only contact was my aunt who called me every few days to talk to me and I could ask her how everyone was.

As the weeks passed by, the overwhelming sense of loss and loneliness became hard to ignore. I started to forget who I really was. I started to wonder if I had made a mistake. I missed mum's face, I missed dad's boasting. I missed the smell of home, the smell of my dad's aftershave and of mum's cooking. My aunt told me that dad had fallen and hurt his knee during one of her many phone calls. He had slipped on ice that had formed in his driveway early one morning. When I put the phone down to my aunt, I sat on my unmade bed and thought of my dad. He used to meticulously prepare the drive with salt the night before if he was told of an impending frost. Our driveway was always frost, snow and ice free- always. And yet he fell. I pictured him, old and vulnerable, slipping and falling on a small amount of ice. I cried for him that day.

Unbeknown to me, my aunt was calling my mum and updating her on how I was getting on. When they all turned up with dad at my door step, I let them in before breaking down and hugging them all. Dad sobbed into my hair as he hugged me so tight, I thought he would never let me go. Mum looked old and tired but this was nothing compared to how my dad looked. He looked like a different person. Old and withered. The grey in his hair had overtaken the black and they had both lost a lot of weight. I made cups of tea for everyone. Mum and dad sat either side of me, each holding one of my hands. We talked for a while about work, about the house, about my cousins, about Daniel and then I broke down. I apologised to them. I told them I was sorry for hurting them. I told them I hated seeing them like this, in tears and looking so vulnerable. They cried with me. Dad took me in his arms again and let me rest my head on his chest whilst mum stroked my hair. Dad told me I was his pride, his joy, the light of his eyes and he couldn't bear not seeing me, not hearing my voice. He said he missed putting the Armani watch on me and taking it off every night to polish. He said both him and mum had slept in my bedroom a number of times when it all became too much. I sobbed listening to him. He told me I had to make a choice between them. I wasn't even angry, I was ready before he had even asked. I nodded, my head still buried somewhere in his chest. My aunt started to pack up my things. I got up to help her. Daniel came through the front door and saw my suitcase sat in the middle of our lounge. I will never forget the way his face changed as he surveyed the scene and drew his conclusions about what was happening. He shouted at my parents and told them they couldn't take me, he told them he would call the police and with that took out his mobile phone. I told him to stop. I said 'It's over, it's never going to work for us, we are just too different.' He wouldn't accept it, he stood there, his shoulders shaking as he sobbed and begged me to stop saying that. He begged me to reconsider. He told me he loved me. That I was his life. That he would not be able to live without me. Mum went to hug him and although he let her for a few seconds he soon pushed her away and screamed at her 'It's all your fault, you just couldn't let her be happy could you?' He said the same things to my aunt and to my dad. He said I had been brainwashed, I was under too much pressure, they were making me choose between a life with him or a life with my entire family. My dad was crying silently and told Daniel that he would never understand what it is like to be part of our community. Dad wished him well and said he would pray for him. I walked out of the house with my case. I got into the car with mum, dad and my aunt and we drove away as Daniel stood leaning towards the front door sobbing.

He never contacted me. Some of my friends emailed me to ask whether I really had returned home and whether it was truly my own decision. Once I confirmed this was the case, the contact gradually fizzled out. I left my phone at Daniel's, I left my photos, my diaries, my everything that connected me to him. It was a clean, fresh break. I spent the next few weeks in numbness at what I had done. At home, no one spoke his name but mum and dad comforted me whenever they found me huddled somewhere sobbing. No one spoke to me about him and whether I missed him, whether he had contacted me- nothing. It was as though he had never existed. My Daniel. My beautiful, wonderful Daniel. I spent the next 14 months surrounded by mum, dad, aunts, uncles and cousins I had not seen for what seemed an eternity. I went to a number of social occasions and heavily involved with organising the wedding of one of my cousins. I even choreographed a Bollywood dance routine for her big day with a number of my cousins.

I was introduced to my husband and felt an attraction towards him immediately. I married him within a year of leaving my old life.

I often wonder what Daniel made of my decision. Whether he thinks I never really loved him, whether I had truly been brainwashed by my parents, whether I was too weak to stand up to the whole world and run away with him. I wonder if he even admitted to himself that we were attempting the impossible. My culture was engrained too deeply in me. Much more deeply than I had ever thought. I knew even then, that I wanted my children to be raised with the cultures, values and traditions that I had been raised with. I knew even then, that I felt uncomfortable when I would think about raising children who had no religion. Unless I, myself, went on a long journey to understand myself, I was not strong enough to do any of this all alone. Daniel would never understand the loneliness that comes with being rejected from your family and an entire community. He would not be able to understand the culture that is deeply engrained and how difficult it is to try and change the core of who you really are. I looked into our future and I saw difficulty, sadness, confusion, loneliness and the eventual breakdown of our relationship.

For you Daniel- I thought of you during the singing ceremonies. I was covered in glittering things and had my hands and feet covered in the most beautiful henna patterns. All the women were singing traditional Indian songs, mum even played on the *dhol,* I had no idea she could play these huge Indian drums. She danced and laughed with everyone else. She cried a lot during the ceremonies. I was blessed by everyone who attended. My cousins put together choreographed dances for me and everyone cheered and clapped. I picked three of the most beautiful outfits I could find to wear on my big day. My outfit for the registry office, my outfit for the wedding and my outfit for the *Valimah,* the celebration marking the day after the wedding night. My registry office outfit was a blue and silver sari. It was beautiful, even the officers in the registry office thought so. My wedding day outfit was a red and gold *lengha,* just like I had imagined it would be as a little girl. I had a large gold necklace with earrings that clipped into my hair, a bindi on my forehead, bangles, rings and bells for my ankles. I felt so beautiful. My makeup was done to perfection and my hair was piled high, filled with jewels and flowers. I sat on the stage of this hall whilst the 1200 guests ate and I thought about you. You would have suited the turban my husband was wearing. You would not have been able to do the *bhangra* dance with your group of friends when you entered the hall like my husband did. He danced with all 12 of his friends to show his happiness at marrying me. Everyone cheered for him and clapped in rhythm to their dancing, they wouldn't have clapped for us Daniel. As guests finished eating, they came onto the stage, one by one to bless us and give us gifts of money. They wouldn't have done that for us Daniel. I thought of you as they led me away from the hall, for the *rukhsati,* the leaving ceremony. My parents sobbed as they slowly walked me out of the hall to the waiting hired white Porsche. My husband was stood there, smiling sympathetically as I sobbed and struggled to keep walking towards him. My parents balanced me. The crowd around us were crying, they felt the pain of the parents who were losing a daughter they had lovingly raised. They wouldn't have cried for us Daniel. I thought of you when I rested my head on the chest of my husband and I sobbed gently for us as my husband comforted me.

That night I pretended to be a virgin and lay there with my eyes closed thinking of you as his mouth found its way around my entire body. In the shower the following morning, I felt that familiar soreness between my legs and I thought of you. My *valimah* outfit was gold and white, you would have loved it. People ate and sang and danced. They wouldn't have danced or sung for us Daniel. I thought of you when I cut my cake, everyone clapped and cheered. My parents cuddled and kissed me. My in laws cuddled and kissed me. They adored me. They wouldn't have adored us Daniel. They wouldn't have kissed and cuddled us.

Life went on for me and I became a mother, a wife and a daughter-in-law. My husband takes me out to new places like the Lake District and I never tell him I have already been with you. I just think of you. I wonder sometimes, what would I say to you if I ever saw you walking down a street? Would we talk or would it be better to pretend we don't know one another?

I made the choice that was right for me, we were never meant to be, the differences between us were too vast. The consequences for me were too severe. I think of you often and silently pray for you, you must laugh at me and my belief in god being the atheist you are, but still I pray for you. I hope you find happiness like I have.

6 FARZANA

Amma.

I think it would be right to say that at one time in my life, when I was a lot younger, I knew exactly what dad wanted from me. I always somehow knew though that things would turn out different for me. I can't explain why but I always felt my life, and the lives of my siblings, were going to be different to the life my mum and dad had led. I knew from an early age that dad wanted me to get married, have children and live a similar life to the one he had lived. He expected me to be the same sort of wife as my mum had been to him. He wanted me to marry an Indian boy, from India, from the family- probably a boy from his side of the family, maybe even someone from mum's side of the family. As we grew into teenagers and mum found some courage to speak up, the topic of marriage nearly always resulted in massive screaming matches amongst my parents, trading the worst accusations and insults they could think of. The issue was that both my parents had immense pressure placed on them from their families left behind in India. Those left behind wanted one of their sons or daughters to marry one of us, and thereby give them the chance of a better life by bringing them to England as our respective spouses. After all, if their child managed to make it to the UK, they would send money back and help the family to continue surviving. It would benefit our parents too because it would mean the pressure to continue financially supporting India would reduce and pass to the new arrival. Mum and dad both wanted us to marry into *their* side of the family. Dad would goad mum and promise her that he would rather cut our throats then let us marry some 'low caste uneducated animal' from her extended family. These remarks from him would make us snigger after all, he was the one who chose to marry mum regardless of her caste yet now, he used this very thing against her. During these slanging matches he would often drag up people who had long since died and accuse them of some atrocity- 'Your dad begged me to marry you, he fell to my feet and begged me, all he wanted was my money' dad would scream. Mum would cry 'Why are you bringing the dead into this? My poor dad, he didn't beg you, you wanted a young girl didn't you? After your first wife left you! She was the clever one, the sensible one, to take everything off you and leave. I am the idiot here, I have served you and your family, cooked and cleaned for you, all of my life, nearly 30 years and what is my reward? Not once, *not once* have you or any of your family said thank you to me, not once have they said thank you. And you, you are the worst, what haven't I done for you? I have done everything for you and you have never once told me I am a good wife. You have never once thanked me! You won't help my family, you have so many people from your family already here, help my family- why won't you help just one person in my family?'

I hated listening to these arguments. During our teenage years, my sisters and I would go into our bedrooms and wait for them to exhaust their insults. The argument normally ended with dad leaving the house and slamming the door shut. The house would shake.

We lived in an old house in a Northern town with a growing Asian community. Both my parents were first generation Indians. Dad arrived decades before mum and found a lady who became the love of his life. Against his parents' wishes, he married her and went onto have 2 boys with her right here in the UK. Like most of the first generation Asian's in Britain at that time, dad sent money back to India to help his family and started the process of getting his sister and his brother into the country too. I hear from mum and others that this turned out to be the downfall of his first marriage. Dad says that he filed for divorce after his first wife tried to stop dad's brother and sister coming across from India. Dad would tell us that his first wife didn't want to help his brother and sister because she wanted all the money he was earning to spend on herself. On makeup and fashion. Mum says that dad's sister, my aunt Nilo, who successfully managed to arrive and stay in the UK thanks to the help of my dad, was a cunning, untrustworthy and generally evil person who caused so much trouble within dad's first marriage that it broke down. Dad's first wife, according to my mum, was independent, educated and employed therefore she had control over finances, she was able to stand up as an equal to dad within the marriage-something which dad's family found distasteful and wrong. 'Women should be demure and at home with the children', 'The man should control the finances', 'Who the hell is she to tell you which members of your family you can or cannot bring to England' and so on. Dad and his first wife's relationship was at breaking point as he continued to send money to India and call over members of his family instead of using the joint earnings to support his sons. One day, after a 12 hour factory shift, he returned to a completely empty house. 'She had even ripped the heater off the wall and taken that' dad would say. In that empty house, dad had his first heart attack aged 48- Unbeknown to him at that time, he would be one of the first patients in England to successfully undergo a triple heart bypass and he would never work again. He would spend the rest of his life on disability living allowance and hand-outs from the government. What followed his surgery was a bitter divorce where his boys gave evidence against him, accusing him of domestic violence, emotional and financial abuse and neglect. As the divorce was being finalised, dad flew to India where he saw my mum, a 16 year old, beautiful young girl from a poorer part of the village and decided he wanted her.

The opportunity presented to my mum's family or more specifically, presented to her dad, was like offering a rope to someone deep in a dark well. It was a lift out of the life in which they lived and the promise of a better life on distant shores. A world away from the intense heat, the open sewers, the mud huts, the cow dung patties decorating the mud and straw walls to a life somewhere new and far away. A life in the West, surrounded by opportunity, healthy white faces, success and modernisation. They were never going to say no I think- who would? A respectable wealthy man from a high caste, who's family you know personally, gives your darling daughter the chance to move away from a dusty forgotten village in India and start a life in England – they had to take it. Regardless of dad's age and his first failed marriage, this was still a wonderful opportunity. No doubt there was strategy behind this decision too. Mum's parents probably hoped that their daughter, once settled in England, would apply for her parents and siblings to join her. They probably hoped she would help her 4 brothers settle in England so they could make a life for themselves too. They probably hoped that once she goes on to bear children, she would arrange for some of her children to marry the children of her brothers and sister. They had their dreams and gave away their beautiful young daughter. Dad's family had the same thoughts too. Here was a young, impressionable, low caste, uneducated girl who would be grateful for the rest of her life for the opportunity. She would do as she was asked to do without argument. She would be submissive, quiet, would never know any better- she would be perfect as a wife, a child bearer, cleaner, cook and a daughter in law.

I still have my moments today when I get upset thinking about my mum as a young girl growing up. She always said she had the most loving childhood with her sister and her brothers. She adored her dad and loved her mum. She would wake with the sun and help her mum prepare breakfast. The men would go off to work and the women would look after the livestock. She remembered playing with baby goats, collecting the eggs from the chickens, throwing stones at the giant guava tree which stood proud in the middle of their courtyard, in an attempt to jostle it into giving up some of its riper fruits. She used to tell me about the fields they ploughed and the river that ran by them. The same river where she used to go to wash the family clothes. 'The technique for washing clothes by a riverside is not a simple dunk and rinse, no no' she would tell me, 'it involves choosing a large rock on which you can perch and ensuring you have a decent sized rock in front you on which to put your clothes. You dunk the clothes in the river and then scrub at them with a bar of soap. Once there is sufficient lather, you then beat the clothes using a rolling pin before dunking them in the river to wash the soap out and then you repeat- that's the proper way of washing clothes.'

She talked about sitting on the flat mud roof of one of their outer buildings where the hens resided watching the passing of another day. She and her sister would watch the orange sun bow out from the sky, giving up the stage for the night ink canvas, scattered with thousands of bright shiny stars. Mum was very beautiful in her youth. Her mother, my grandmother, was a fair skinned, blue eyed beauty and was probably a descendant of Alexander the Great- that was the rumour. My grandfather was a handsome man, tall and well-built with an air of humility around him, kind, gentle, brown eyes and a warm touch. When granddad really smiled at you, his eyes shone and danced like amber stones catching the light. The Indian sun had coloured his skin a dark, honey brown and the laugh lines around his eyes and mouth exhumed warmth and kindness. He was a good man. He treated his wife with respect and loved his children. He had a respectable job in the army as a cleaner. He earned an income which made him better than others in his village. He had done well for someone born into his caste and did not have to resort to begging like other families in the village. The poverty still existed for him though. They could afford meat twice a month only and lived off a diet of rice, lentils, eggs and *chappatis*. Mum would tell me about the morning *parathas* they would occasionally make. *Parathas* are like a *chapatti* but a more luxurious version. When making a paratha, you need to pick up more than your normal amount of dough which you separate into two smaller pieces. You then add *ghee* to both the smaller pieces before joining them back together. The trick is to position the *ghee* in the middle of the dough ball to start with so when you are rolling the dough out into a circular shape, you would also be spreading the *ghee*. Once this *ghee* laden chapatti hits the piping hot *tava*, it sizzles as the dough and ghee cook together forming crunchy parts and softer doughy parts. The end result is a crispy, blackened in parts, salty paratha which would be served up with sweet eggs. Sweet eggs were just that- scrambled eggs made with butter and sugar. When they are served with piping hot *parathas* they are gorgeous. The sweet, soft egg against the hot, crispy, salty paratha, eaten in the cold of the dawn before the sun rises and begins baking the earth.

Everything was cooked on a traditional stove then, a three sided, lidless cube made of mud and stone within which one added wood, fire and dry cow dung. Once the flames had started, you added your stove or your pot and started cooking. Mum remembers how once cooking had finished and the fire was dying, she would bury the smallest potatoes into the ashes and leave them there to cook as the family ate together. Once the evening dishes were cleared away, both sisters would eat the tiny little baked potatoes whilst sharing stories about the fairies who lived by the river. And the witch who came from the other side of the river and possessed a young woman from the village who had to be exorcised. It was a simple peaceful life.

When I think of her life then I see it in my mind as a clean piece of crisp white paper. Smooth, unmarked, simple, creaseless and pure yet when I think of her life only a few years ago, that paper is crumpled, ripped and has black incoherent scribbles all over it. She has never spoken about her actual wedding day to any of us except to say that she thought she was marrying dad's younger brother. Dad was at that point, 36 years older than mum. He was 52 and mum was 16. Regardless of who she thought she was marrying, mum would not have the option of picking one over the other. The decision had already been made that she would marry dad and that was the end of any discussion there might have been. She must have found out on her wedding day who her groom to be really was. She has never spoken about her wedding day to any of us. In some parts of India, it is still common to not know who you are marrying until the ceremony starts to take place. I have no idea what her wedding dress looked like, what jewellery she wore or what her make-up was like but I imagine it to be simple and plain. What mum did talk to us about was what happened when she left India for England. She speaks about how she sobbed into her father's chest, terrified at the prospect of getting onto an aeroplane. She didn't trust the machine and couldn't understand how metal was able to fly. I remember her telling me the story of her arriving at this 'huge airport' - Gatwick. She arrived wearing a tight, bright pink and gold *shalwar kameez*, complete with a light pink organza veil, was covered with golden embroidery and gold high heeled shoes. She was wearing her wedding gold, big gold earrings, a gold necklace and a full set of gold bangles. 'I jingled every time I took a step! If it wasn't the jewellery, it was the sound of my ankle bells against my gold high heels. On top of that, your grandmother gave me a big tub of *ghee* because your dad liked it so much and apparently you couldn't buy it in England and so I had to carry that along with my suitcase. Can you imagine? This tall, skinny girl, drenched in bright pink and gold, carrying a metal container of *ghee,* walking round and around this huge airport looking for your dad?'

Eventually security took an interest in her and quickly realised she couldn't speak a word of English and was new to the UK. 'I was frightened of these *gorey,* their blue eyes and pale skin, one *gora*, this big man with bushy eyebrows and a bushy beard was really nice to me. Another *goree* with light gold hair was also nice to me. She kept touching my gold jewellery and my long black hair.' They put mum in a hostel with other females from different

116

parts of the world. 'There were some other Indian women in the hostel so I was able to talk to them and eat with them but I was frightened. I was there for 4 days before I saw your dad. I had to stay there for over 2 weeks. I cried every single night. When I think back to then I laugh sometimes, I guarded that tub of *ghee* with my life! I wasn't so worried about the gold or my high shoes, just the *ghee* for your dad'. It turned out that the decree nisi from dad's first marriage had not been finalised and when dad's first wife heard he had remarried, she went to the police to report a crime. In the fortnight that mum spent in the hostel, dad agreed to give his first wife everything she asked for – half the house, half their savings, half of everything. In the rare moments when dad talks about those times, he always paints himself as a hero- the guy who gave *half* of all his wealth to his ex-wife. The community, family and even mum, paint him as a hero; 'She took everything from him you know, and he gave it all away for me, so he could come and pick me up from the airport. I was so happy when that day came. I remember the evenings on the days he was allowed to visit me. They would only allow him to visit for 2 hours every evening so after they asked him to leave, he would sit in his car, outside my window, and we would look at each other for hours. I would wave to him sometimes and then fall asleep at the window watching his outline in the car as dusk fell.' Dad had applied for a council house and this was mum's first home in England. A house made of brick not mud, with carpets and heat spread by central heating and not the Indian sun. 'I had to learn how to use a hoover, the taps, the fridge, the freezer and the shower- I hated the shower. I couldn't get used to the force of the water. I used to have baths. I didn't understand how the *gorey* would actually clean their skins. In India we used to find the best flat pumice stones and scrub ourselves to get rid of the dirt, here they use soaps and creams when they bathe - how is that cleaning yourself? Mind you, they are quite white aren't they, they can't have much dirt on them to start with.'

The neighbours were also Asian - Pakistani, Bengali and Indian all lived on the same estate as mum and dad alongside some white British families. 'I remember when we went to a supermarket, I couldn't believe how everything was kept... Everything was in small packets, all sealed or boxed or in the refrigerator. The fruit piled up high and all the sweet things- so many sweet things. I also couldn't believe the cost. I was astonished at how much apples cost compared to India, everything seemed to cost ten times more. I remember seeing all the colours on all the items and the different symbols. Of course, I couldn't read or write English and had little idea of what I might find in a sealed packet or a box. The fruit was simple enough but I remember once going out, by myself, to pick some crisps. I know now that they are Walkers crisps but back then, I had to rely on the colours and the pictures. Your dad really liked the salty ones so I went out once, by myself, and bought the biggest bag I could find. I was so surprised by the honesty of the cashiers, I thought it was amazing how they always gave me change and never tried to barter with me. The prices were on a white sticker on the item although it took me years to understand what the numbers meant. The big bag I took home for your dad well, they turned out to be a variety bag and contained bacon and beef flavoured crisps! That was that! Your father was disgusted! He marched over to the *goras* house, 3 doors down, and threw the crisps into their garden for their children to eat.'

Dad wasn't as educated as he liked to tell people. Later in life he would berate mum 'You are so stupid, you illiterate piece of shit. You and your dumb family, you were always the village idiots. You can't read or write, you have nothing but hay between your ears.' To this day, dad hasn't realised that flavouring crisps doesn't mean they contain animal products- the crisps were still fine for vegetarian consumption. It still makes me smile when I think of him, striding across to the neighbours and flinging bacon flavoured crisps into their back yard, as though that was a normal thing to do. Mum remembers the first few years of her marriage as being wonderful. 'Your dad was so good to me, he would take me to Blackpool almost every week.' I think there was a time in his life when dad loved my mum. Whether that was the same love he had for his first wife, we will never know. He cared for her, and loved her enough to go on and father 7 children with her.

When I think about their lives, I cannot ignore the correlation between their relationship rotting and mum becoming more independent and knowledgable on the ways of the western world. She started learning about numbers when we were at primary school and were able to teach her. I remember mum repeating the numbers 1-10 back to us and pointing to them on the phone she would use to call India. The phone we had then was a giant, yellowy coloured phone with huge square buttons on the front. In hindsight, the phone and the comically large numbers and buttons were fantastic for mum. Someone had written down the number of the local telephone centre in India for her on a scrap of paper. She would carefully take out this scrap and match the written symbols to the buttons on the phone allowing her to make a call. Calling India in the 80's and 90's was a long affair because the rural villagers did not have access to a phone. There would be one phone a few miles away owned either by a richer family or by a phone office- a local business. *They* would answer your incoming call and take a message. A runner, typically a child, would then relay the message to the family concerned who would travel to wherever the device was and wait for a second call. I remember mum ringing India and talking to whoever answered the phone, requesting that they get her mother and father to come to the phone.

The person on the other end would say to call back in half an hour. Mum would call back in half an hour and voila! She would have a conversation with her family over a crackling line with a delay of about 3 seconds on either end. Sometimes mum would pass the phone to us and we would speak too. I used to get frustrated at the delay. I would always be mid-sentence asking them the obligatory 'How are you all doing?' when a voice would cut in with 'Hello? Hello? Is that you? You sound all grown up.' I would stop talking and start replying 'Yes, yes I am fine how'.....before they would answer my original question 'Oh yes, yes we are all fine, it is very hot today.'

Mum was able to ring India every week using a phone card which was preloaded with minutes and came in denominations starting at £5. I do not know what she did in the earlier years when we were toddlers but I like to believe that dad helped her make the calls and gave her the phone cards or the money to buy them. Dad never allowed her to have driving lessons or attend college for English lessons, he did not see how that would be a good thing. He encouraged his sister, Nilo, to attend college and to take driving lessons but then, she was his sister and as dad would always say, 'Nilo is very intelligent, she is after all, my sister.'

Mum latched onto the Asian community around her, making friends with older females who took pity on her. She was 'unfortunate' they would tell her, because she had no family here. She was also 'unfortunate' because she had married dad and everyone knew about dad and the arrogance of his family, the arrogance of his high caste. Mum learnt a lot through the community; where to buy particular spices and meats from, how to use public telephone boxes, where things were, what fish and chips were and what some of her entitlements were. The only money she had was an allowance that dad would give her every week. Mum had no knowledge of bank accounts or benefits or child support allowance- dad knew all of that. He set up joint accounts and had sole control of them. He would give mum a few pounds each week with which she was to feed, clothe and buy necessities. In the earlier years, mum and dad would go shopping together but that changed over the decades and shopping solo became the norm. Dad had control over what mum could buy in those earlier days. He always exercised control when he had to pay for the shopping, often by taking things back to shelves and not buying enough meat for everyone- just enough for him. Mum had no bank account and had no documents to prove her identity even if she wanted her very own account. Dad 'looked after' all of her documents including her passport. There were arguments whenever mum asked for her personal documents to open a bank account. Dad wanted to know why she needed her own account. Did she have money to save? If so, he was obviously giving her too much. Mum decided to stop approaching him eventually and instead, spoke to people in the community. They were her saving grace. To this day, mum still uses *kameti* – an interest free loan and saving scheme run by members of the community. *Kameti* has been life changing for hundreds of thousands of females suffering from financial abuse. It works like this: A set number of people take part and they have to commit, verbally, to giving the leader of the *kameti* a set amount of money over a set period of time. Each individual partaking is assigned a number, via a draw, which determines your position within the group and when you will receive your lump sum. So there could be a *kameti* for £1200, with 12 women taking part which is scheduled to run for 12 months. Each individual has to input £100 every month by a specific date, giving the leader £1200 cash every month. The person who is then drawn as number 1 will be the first to receive this £1200 cash but, they have to continue making payments of £100 for the full 12 months. In month 2, the person who drew the second number will receive the second £1200. As they will have already given £100 they will need to continue repaying £100 per month for the next 11 months. When the *kameti* finishes in month 12, everyone will have given £1200 and also taken £1200. The number you draw in the kameti is very flexible too. There have been times when mum has taken part in a *kameti* and needed the money straight away, in month 1. In these cases she was able to swap her number with another member of the group taking part in the *kameti*. There have also been times when mum has drawn the 3rd or 4th number but has not needed the money so soon and has therefore swapped her number with another lady who did need the money more urgently. This method allowed her to save money. Decades later, mum took part in a £10,000 kameti over a period of 5 years paying about £170 per month. She used her *kameti* money to pay for my eldest sisters marriage having foreseen that dad was not going to part with his money that easily. Her first kameti was very humble. It was saving £50, then £70 then £100 and so on. She was able to save £2.50 per week from the money dad gave her and put this into her first ever *kameti* when we were still children. When she received her £50, she bought new cutlery, dishes and a food processor for the kitchen. Businesses, owned by Asian men to serve predominantly the Asian community, started to appear and were a blessing for mum and countless other females in her situation. It was, and today still is, extremely normal for Asian shop owners to let people from their community take an item and pay for it on instalments. No paperwork or interest, just a verbal contract. Mum bought a lot of household goods from these stores- toasters, frying pans, dishes and trinkets, paying for them either with *kameti* money or by giving the store owner a few pounds per month. She didn't personally know these people but they were part of the community and therefore they looked after one of their own. They would address her as 'sister' or 'daughter' and with the utmost respect. I don't know what mum would have done without *kameti*'s or without such businesses or the community presence. The community was a place you loved and a place that helped you.

It was also a place you hated, a place which kept you bound to it and punished you if you strayed. Your honour is everything within the community and opportunities only come your way *if* you have honour. You can partake in *kameti*'s if you have honour and you can have a wide social circle if you have honour. There are also expectations within the community you need to adhere to if you want your position within this community to remain. An example of this is being invited to an Indian wedding. We were invited to one wedding I remember and our relationship to the bride? Well, in India, my mum's family knew the cousin of the bride for he was the village tailor. That is how we knew them and they knew us. The etiquette and unwritten community rule is that once you have an invitation to a wedding, which you accept and attend, then when the time arrives for you to throw a wedding, you will return the favour and invite them. This doesn't just end with invites. When you are invited to a wedding, you gift money to the bride or groom – presents tend to be a no although this is changing with the second and third generation Asians. There is always an elderly female who sits with the happy couple and has a small book, in which she makes notes on who attended and how much money they gifted. Inviting 800 people to an Indian wedding is normal; you can recoup £16,000 if everyone gifts £20 to the bride and groom. You can also rest in the knowledge that whatever you gift at this wedding, you will receive back from that same family when you host a wedding. I remember mum telling us all about a lady called Shameem who, when her daughter was getting married, was given £20 by Aunt Farzana, a friend of mums. A good, generous amount. Years later, when Shameem attended the wedding of Aunt Farzana's daughter however, she only gifted the happy couple £5. Well, there was outrage! The community talked about Shameem in hushed tones and hints were dropped to members of Shameem's extended family about her, her insolence and lack of community spirit: 'When *her* daughter got married, everyone gave her £20, £30 and look at her, the greedy woman, £5?! Who gives £5? What are they going to do with £5?!' She wasn't invited to many weddings after that. The community was a contradiction, an enigma wrapped in confusion and custom. It had good and ugly points. There were always rumours floating around in the community, in the mosques and during social gatherings about how a wife, a sister, a niece or a daughter had succumbed to the ways of the west. 'Well, he should never have allowed her to have driving lessons you know, that's when she started to spoil. She then wanted to learn English and before you knew it, she ran off with another man!' or 'Well, they sent her to college didn't they for an 'education' what a great education she had in getting pregnant and running away! The poor dad can't even make eye contact with anyone anymore and the poor mum? Well, she is so ill. I don't think she even gets out of bed anymore, just prays for death- oh *tauba tauba*.' I remember as a child, seeing people say *tauba tauba* whilst touching their ears with their fingers and shaking their head, side to side, at the same time. *Tauba* meant to repent, you would use these words and actions when you heard something which you found to be obscene, unbecoming and wrong. A female running away and disgracing the family warranted a *tauba tauba*, a female caught with a boyfriend warranted a *tauba tauba*, a female who cut her hair too short warranted a *tauba tauba*, a female who wore red lipstick and was not at a wedding or getting married warranted a *tauba tauba*, a really fat man, white people kissing on the TV, seeing a white woman in a mini skirt on a hot day- these were all good reasons to say *tauba tauba*. Seeing an Asian girl wearing a mini skirt would warrant a much more vigorous *tauba tauba* and would include gasps, open mouths and even a dizzy spell.

My aunt Nilo had married from India and now had a husband and 4 children of her own. Mum had 5 girls at this point and was heavily pregnant with a 6th. The constant pregnancies were not born purely out of lust but more in the hope of bearing a boy. Mum and dad both really wanted a boy. They had 5 girls and everyone knew that girls were strangers. Girls would always go to another man one day, to another family but boys, boys were family property and would bring in a wife, earn money and look after the parents. My parents would get their wish of a boy during Mum's 6th pregnancy - something which prompted a 7th impregnation but not with the same success- a 6th girl. Dad was 68 when his youngest daughter was born. Mum cooked and cleaned a lot. Aunt Nilo, uncle Muhammed and their children would be over most afternoons and evenings. We would all eat, talk and play together whilst mum served food and cleaned up around everyone. Aunt Nilo would keep mum company and viewing this from a child eyes, things seemed good between them. I remember the stories aunt Nilo would tell us, like the one about the handsome couple who wanted a boy. They had 4 girls and really, desperately wanted a boy. One night, a fairy came to the woman and said to her to go to the mango tree in her courtyard at dawn, and eat the mango from the middle of the tree. The woman was gluttonous and had already eaten a large amount at dinner. When dawn broke, she went to the courtyard and there it was, a golden mango, right in the middle of the tree. She snatched it and started to guzzle on it. She was already full from the dinner and only managed to eat half of this mango. She noticed there were many other ripe mangoes on the tree and so threw away the half she could not manage. Nine months later she gave birth to a boy just like they had hoped for but, it was half a boy. He only had one eye, one nostril, one arm and one leg. We were enthralled by this story, we would ask 'What? Really? What about his bellybutton? Did he only have half a belly button?' There were many adventures that this half boy borne from a mango had and we spent many Sunday evenings listening to aunt Nilo tell us. Mum never told us stories, she was always cooking for us all, or cleaning or changing nappies. She would look after aunt Nilo's 4 children too. She would bathe them, feed them and change them too. The abuse which was always present in my parents' relationship did rear its head on occasions for all of us to bear witness to. I remember one Winters morning at the age of 7, I was getting ready to leave for school. I ran downstairs and came across dad screaming at my mum who stood cowering in the corner of the room. Grandma was staying with us, visiting from India. She was sat on the floor, by the fire as always and was watching my mum cower with interest. Dad continued to scream at her and mum continued to cower. She was cradling her head, burying her face into her arms and her body was slowly curling into a foetal position. She was sobbing. Grandma shouted 'Tell her my boy, tell her. Remind her of her place' and with that, dad picked up the cup and saucer holding his tea and hurled them at mum. The cup smashed against the brick wall that was covered only by a thin layer of paint, and the hot tea drenched mums *shalwaar* scalding her thighs and legs. 'What are you looking at' dad barked at me 'Go on, get off to school.' Later that morning, during my first break in school, I started to cry. I still don't know what had transpired that morning between mum, dad and grandma. I just remember the smashed saucer and cup. Mum had bought and paid for that tea set on instalments, it was a beautiful set, matte white in colour with gold edging and red roses adorning the cups. She was so proud of herself for being able to save enough money and own something which was truly hers. I remember mums light pink *shalwaar kameez,* which she had sewn by herself, drenched in tea. I remembered her glossy black hair, which had become loose, cascading down her shoulders, hiding her face. I remember the look on my grandma's face, a look that exhumed satisfaction and hardness.

Mum was still adapting to the western world a decade on. Our old council house on Minshull street was large but dark and damp. Some of the walls had no insulation or plaster, they were just bricks covered with a thin coat of paint. The house was crooked and oddly shaped. As you entered through the front door, you stood in the landing which a small square. To the right there was a room we termed the 'front room' and to the left was the living room. Straight ahead was the narrow staircase which led to a bathroom and 2 bedrooms. I remember the front room well, it was always kept locked and the key stored in the living room. There was a large glass locked cabinet, a plush grey fabric sofa, a TV on a stand and a coffee table. This room was only ever used for praying and for when we had guests. It was always immaculate. The living room was always warm` mum always had the gas fire on. The carpets were a deep red and brown colour and the sofa's were green. There was another TV, a coffee table and access to the small room under the stairs which housed our coats, shoes and anything else it could take. By walking through the living room, and via a high concrete step and a glass door you could access the very narrow and crooked kitchen. Connected to the kitchen was another door leading to the back garden which was in reality a small square of grey concrete. Mum would sometimes bathe us in the garden as young girls. We would have to strip to our underwear and she would use the cold water via a hosepipe to wash us. We were given large pumice stones to scrub ourselves with. I remember the bitterness of winter, the biting cold, the first gasp we would take when the cold water would hit our goose pimpled skin and how lovely it felt to be back inside the house wrapped in a towel, all of us fighting to get as close as possible to the burning fire. That's how mum used to bathe in India and so I suppose it was normal for her. She always said our skin looked cleaner, whiter after a cold garden bath. There were 3 bedrooms upstairs and one bathroom. Mum and dad had a room within which were crammed 1 single and 2 double beds. Dad had 1 of the double beds for himself, mum would share her double bed with the youngest of us. The next youngest would sleep in the single bed. The rest of us were crammed into the remaining rooms, sharing either double beds or using bunk beds. We didn't have much to play with. Dad would visit car boot sales on Sundays and sometimes, he would take mum and us along too. He would buy us the toys he could afford. I remember when we got a deck of cards once, we would play 'snap' most evenings and end up fighting over the cards. My older sister was a terrible cheat- she would just snatch the pile of cards, or place her card down really quickly whilst screaming 'SNAAAAP SNAAAP' before snatching the pile of cards up and claiming them as hers. Chaos would often ensue and we would roll around, howling with laughter until we were scolded by mum. 'Caaaaaw caaaw caaaaw, you are all like crows, is this how girls should be? Have you eaten crows today?' That used to make us laugh more- who eats crows? We didn't get spending money from dad, he used to get angry if we asked him for any. We used to sit around for hours sometimes, dreaming up the courage to ask him for money when there was a school trip. Frequently, we would ask mum to ask him on our behalf and she would have to bear his moods and his questions. Dad was well respected at our local mosque, he was well known for giving his money to charity and for raising funds for charitable causes. In our front room, in the glass cabinet, we had some gold coloured, glass goblets, cups, saucers and plates which had arrived from India, a tin collection box full of money and a horsewhip. The cabinet was padlocked and dad would keep the key on his person all the time. I somehow learnt how to unpick the lock on this cabinet and get the tin out which contained collection money. I could not get into the box itself but, I could turn it upside down and poke and prod the slit through which you would deposit your coins, cajoling them out. I found that a wooden stick, the only remnant of an ice lolly and a hair pin were the best tools for this job although anything sturdy which fitted the coin slot worked well too. This became a regular activity for me. On some days I would manage a few bronze coins and collect 10 pence, other days I be fortunate enough to tease out a pound. I had to be quick and quiet, the rattling of the money made a lot of noise so I had to use a cushion to muffle the noise whenever I tilted the box. I spent the money on sweets and shared these with my sisters, never telling them the truth about how the sweets were acquired. The day I got caught is the first clear memory I have of being whipped. I remember feeling scared when dad started banging on the front room door (I locked it whenever I was taking money), shouting at me to unlock the door. I had the charity box upside down under a pillow and the cabinet was wide open. Before letting dad in, I had to turn the box upright, put it back into the cabinet and lock the cabinet, all whilst remaining as silent as possible. Of course, he must have heard the noise of the tin and the jangling of the coins. He came in and surveyed the room, I stared hard at the ground. He told me to sit, pointing to the sofa. I knew right then what was about to happen. He went to the cabinet, took out his keys, examined the padlock before unlocking it, examined the collection box closely and then reached for the whip. The whip itself was about 22 inches in length, flexible and a matt black in colour. There was a piece of solid silver metal on one end. On researching the whip now, it seems it was a 'show cane', used during show jumping events with horses. It made a terrifying whooshing noise through the air, a noise that still frightens me today. I started to cry, mum came rushing in and my sisters were trying to peer into the room from behind mum. 'What are you doing? What has she done?' mum asked. 'It's none of your concern what YOUR daughter has done' dad replied, 'get out, all of you right now, get out.' Mum stood at the doorway for a few seconds, I knew there was nothing she could do. She left taking my sisters with her and closing the door. Dad locked the door and started to whip me. I curled up into a ball, sobbing and crying out at the pain of each lash. When he had finished, he sat on the sofa next to the one I was curled up on. I sobbed until I fell asleep there. I was awoken by dad stroking my hair, he gently told me to get up and go into the living room. I did as I was told. I wonder if felt guilt for his actions then? Maybe that's why he was so tender towards me after. He must have felt it to be a difficult task, to father us they way he thought he should. To father us the way he had been raised, to father us the way his culture told him to raise daughters.

I remember one evening when dad came back from the mosque and collapsed on the sofa. I was 12 then and we were watching Saturday night television, sat on the floor on our old, tired looking carpet. Dad picked up the remote and turned the TV off. Immediately we all turned around to face him, mum look concerned. Dad said 'I have just heard the worst news in the mosque. I feel sick just talking to you about it but I have to keep you girls safe. I must tell you this. There are lots of bad girls out there now you know? They will lead you astray. Doctor Khan gave a speech to us all in the mosque tonight and told us about the number of *our* Asian girls going to the surgery to him, to the other doctors and asking for these tablets because they have boyfriends. They ask for abortions, killing a baby because they have had boyfriends. The dirty prostitutes. *Tauba tauba tauba*, I feel sick when I think about this, what is happening to us in the world? Our girls, our pure, beautiful girls are being led astray. They will go straight to hell when the day of judgement comes and will burn there. Girls, you must continue to pray to Allah so he protects you. I pray for you all the time. All of you, I pray for you, I pray for all of you all the time' and with that he sobbed. We all rushed up to him, hugged him and made promises to him that we would never do that, we would never do such bad things, we are not like that, we are good girls, we will never wear skirts or have boyfriends or cut our hair or wear make up or go out and that he needn't worry about us. Unbeknown to me at that time, my eldest sister who was 16, promptly changed her doctor, who was Dr Hussain, and started to go and see the white doctor who had a surgery about half an hour away.

As we blossomed into women, things became worse between mum and dad. We started to stick up for mum as we continued to witness and understand the utter injustice of her situation, her existence. Her wonderful father was taken ill in India. He was diagnosed with cancer and given months to live. Mum was desperate to go but dad would not allow it. He said he needed her to stay with him, to look after him and did not have the money to pay for her ticket. We were working, young women by then and so over the next few months, we saved our wages and were able to buy her a ticket. Once dad found out that we had funded her airfare *and* given her enough money to last out there for a few weeks, he was delirious with rage. He banned her from leaving the house. Although we were all in our late teenage years or in our early twenties by then, we were still controlled by dad and still very much afraid of his wrath and of any consequences that might arise from challenging him. He had such a hold over us all. Whenever we challenged him strongly, he would feign heart trouble. Our memories were still scarred from an incident a few years ago when one my sisters, having witnessed dad slap mum, pushed him back before punching him to the floor. It caused him to have a heart attack and spend nearly a week in hospital. This guilt never left my sister and the entire incident was burnt into all of our minds. None of us wanted to risk the chance of being labelled as the daughter who killed her father, that label would be too difficult to live with. There were other occasions when, as we became older, more educated and independent, we would challenge dad or overrule him on something. We would back our mum in the latest argument, often over finances. Dad would respond by sulking. He would stop talking to all of us. He would stop eating or sitting with us. He would stop buying food for the house and stop paying bills. We had our phone service cut off on numerous occasions. We would have weeks of this sort of behaviour from him. He would leave the house in the morning and not return until the evening. On the rare occasions when he returned home during an afternoon, he would sit in the front room, away from us all. During the first few decades, it was mum who broke first and would pander to his needs, asking him if he wanted something to eat or drink. She would continue asking the questions even when she had no response from him, even when he would tell her to shut up and go away. Even when he would throw any food she had prepared for him against the walls. As we became accustomed to this behaviour, we stopped asking him how he was or whether he wanted anything. This resulted in dad taking his game up a notch. He would moan and groan in the evenings before staggering to the bathroom. We would all sit and listen to him crawling in pain to the bathroom and then hearing the door shut. He would then crawl from the bathroom, on his hands and knees, making enough noise for at least one of us to break- usually mum first. We would rush to his aid and help him up and onto the sofa. We would go to the bathroom and see the red in the toilet bowl. Initially we were petrified that he had something terribly wrong with him. That soon stopped after we found the small pot of red food colouring hidden behind the toilet. We had seen too many of these acts, we had seen mum kept imprisoned for too long. Mum found some strength from somewhere and with us backing her, she continued to pack and get ready to leave for India to see her sick father. I drove her to the airport myself. As we waited for the checking in desk to open, mum told me she felt guilty for leaving dad in this manner and without his consent. I got a call from my sister who had stayed at home to keep an eye on dad. She told me dad had suffered a heart attack and the ambulance had taken him. As soon as I heard the words I knew mum would break. I wish I had never told her but I did. I was right, mum turned and walked out of the airport and we returned home. The doctors told us they suspected dad had suffered some mild angina and thus upped his medication. My grandfather died two weeks later. I never forgave him for that. I thought about pushing him down the stairs, beating him until his heart finally gave up and contemplated murder during my own times of rage towards him. Three years later, mum's family called to say that grandmother was seriously ill. She had been ill for weeks and mums sister had been calling most days, begging mum to travel to India so they could be together during this difficult time. Mum wasn't convinced at the severity of her mothers' illness. Well, that's what she told people when they questioned her decision to not go to India right away. The truth was that dad again, had said no. He told her she was not allowed to go. He had her passport hidden away somewhere. We all tried to get her passport, we pleaded with him, we begged him and threatened him- nothing worked. When mum got another call from her heartbroken sister telling her that the doctors had given their mother days to live, mum fell to dad's feet asking for her passport. She begged him and reminded him that he had stopped her seeing her own father years ago and to not do this injustice again. Dad still refused. He said he needed her to remain here, to look after him. He was old now and she could not just go off for a few weeks to India when she had responsibilities here. We were aghast. I went to hit him. The rage, pent up from all those years of watching him walking all over my poor mother was too much. I had my hands around his throat and I was squeezing with all my might. I wanted to feel his neck break in my hands. I was overcome with blind rage and loathing and continued to squeeze. My sisters and my mother managed to pry my fingers off his withered neck and dragged me away from him, utterly enraged with me. They all screamed at me demanding to know what in god's name I was thinking. Mum rushed to dad to check if he was ok, of course, he wasn't. I had made things worse. I had given him the perfect platform on which he could show us all his acting skills once more. And oh boy he did not fail us. He cried bitterly, wailed and beseeched forgiveness for whatever sin he had committed, it must have been a grave sin to warrant this treatment and from his own daughter! His own flesh and blood! He grasped at his chest and feigned a heart attack. He spent one night in hospital being monitored. He told the doctors, nurses, anyone who would listen about his ungrateful daughter and how she had tried to kill him. We turned the house upside down to try and find mum's passport but did not succeed. I wanted to go to the police but my mum, angry at my insolence and for raising a hand at her husband warned me against it. So strong was her loyalty and so afraid of the consequences, she still backed him. He returned home on a Wednesday morning. On that very evening, as he tucked into the lamb curry and *chappatis* mum had made and served to him, another phone call from India informed us that grandma had died. How bitterly my mum sobbed sat all alone in England.

How it must have felt for my wonderful grandmother, laying on her death bed, waiting for her youngest daughter to arrive. Her daughter who left her at the age of 16. Her daughter who she had not laid eyes on for over 10 years. How it must have felt for mum, knowing that her only opportunity of a final goodbye to her own mother had been snatched so cruelly from her. I thought about her sat with her mother as a little girl, eating those salty *paratha's* in the cold of the morning. I thought about her as a little girl, having her hair combed and coaxed into submission by her mum. I thought about her poor mum and the heartache she must have felt watching her tall, thin, teenage daughter leave for a foreign country and a life abroad with a new man. I wonder if she was ever happy at the decision. I thought about her father and the times he must have picked mum up as a little girl, swinging her through the air before kissing her head, his eyes dancing with joy. I thought about the little dolls that Mum and her sister would make as little girls and sew clothes for. I sobbed with my mum for everything she had lost.

I wished death on dad that day. I wished him death because only in his death would mum be free. I always admired mum for the countless lies she told her family whenever they called from India. They would ask why she wasn't visiting and she would say her husband isn't well. They would ask why she hadn't called for weeks, why they couldn't get through when they called and she would say they have had trouble with the telephone lines. She would never tell them dad hit her. She would never tell them that dad stopped paying the phone bills resulting in the service being cut. She would never tell them that he gives her an allowance to live off or has taken her passport away from her.

Dad let her weep. He consoled her as he ate his curry, sat on the table with his back to all of us. He consoled her with his words 'Don't cry too much now, death is a part of life. She was a good woman but we all return to the ground from where we came.'

I hate the word cunt. I detest it. But I wanted to shout that word as loud as I could. It was the worst word I could think of in any language. I wanted to scream that word at him, repeat it again and again until my vocal chords exploded. But I sat with my sisters, surrounded mum, and we cried quietly together.

She was shackled to him through tradition, customs, culture, fear, duty and love and we, us modern strong educated girls, we were shackled to mum through our love for her. Where I wanted to pack his things and throw him out into the street, my mother would cry and beg me to not do anything as such because it would hurt her. We were inside this prison where the lock keeping us there, keeping us imprisoned, was our father.

I wanted her to leave him but she wouldn't listen. She said she would not be able to take the shame that came with walking out on an old husband. Dad must have felt completely out of control in his final years. He was physically weak and could not hit her anymore, he would have to contend with all of us. He couldn't shout as loud as he wanted, I shouted louder than him. He couldn't try and tell me that culturally, women should stay at home, my arguments were stronger than his. Education is such a wonderful thing. It gave us sisters the power to be able to sit together and discuss mum and dad. He hated it when we would stand by our mum. He wanted us to be like him, agree with his treatment of women, his beliefs and his outlook on life. He even said to us we were not like our mum, she was stupid and illiterate, we were educated like him and strong minded, like him. He hated it when in these situations we would smile at him and say absolutely nothing. Our silence at these statements could not be interpreted as an agreement, it was in fact complete disagreement but done in a respectful manner and he knew it. As we became more independent he became more powerless and more desperate to regain that power. We were able to understand that by losing his power at home, he was becoming agitated. When he became agitated he took his anger out on his wife. We understood that we needed to placate him and make him feel like he was in control of all of us and so we did. We would sit with him, listening to him as he would talk about the situation in Iran, his hate for the Shi'ate Muslims and their loopy tradition of self-flagellation. We would nod with him at his solutions of a better India and their right to Kashmir. We would nod along when he would tell us about the latest woman stoned to death for adultery and how she deserved it for besmirching her family's honour. Us sisters became rocks for each other. We would call one other and say, 'Just spent the day with dad and I am seething, I need to let off steam.' That would be followed by a full debrief, general anger, ranting, deep breaths and then calm.

Life then does not seem real to me anymore. I see myself as a child and can't recognise that little girl. We all changed so much as we completed school, college and fought to go to university. Both of my older sisters were forced into marriages and both left their husbands after years of violence. They both live in their own council houses with their children and get through the days somehow. Dad blamed them for the breakdown of their respective marriages, right until the day he died. Mum never said a word.

I think often of my dad and how it must have felt knowing your daughters despise your teachings. I wonder if he ever thought he was unfair to my mother? Whether he stopped in the cold light of day and knew, in his heart, that his actions against mum were cruel? I wonder how often he thought of his first wife. I wonder if he felt guilty for his actions? I wonder if he regretted his decision to leave his first wife and whether his decision was based on his honour and his pride? Everyone told him he needed to teach her a lesson, she was too independent earning her own money, too independent having driving lessons, disrespectful for keeping her earnings and disrespectful for doing what she wanted to do. I wonder if he ever missed her or felt it was wrong when he went to India to marry a child. Did he ever feel guilty for snatching mum from her own family and bringing her to England where she became his personal slave? I wonder if he was ever sorry for the suffering he caused her. For the suffering he caused all of us.

Life is better for mum now that dad has finally died. We found out what a strong swimmer she is from her friends who told us all one evening when we were visiting. The local swimming pool has a ladies only evening and mum started to attend every week with her friends after dad died. Most of the Asian women swam in trousers and shirts but my mum would wear a swimming costume. I felt so proud of her for being able to do that and I felt so happy for her knowing she had the freedom to wear a swimming costume in a swimming pool surrounded by ladies only. At first she just got used to the limited area she had in which to swim but after a few weeks, she was swimming length after length. Mum told us all that when she was much younger, she and her sister would swim in the river that ran behind their parents' house. The current was strong and once, she was washed away, down the river, eventually pulled out by women washing their clothes a few miles away. My heart was bursting with joy for her. How it must have felt for her, to have that freedom to swim again. That freedom she lost at the age of 16 when she arrived in England.

Today she is leaving for India. It has been 3 years since her mother passed away and 13 years since she last saw her sister and her brothers. All us sisters decided to pay for her airfare and give her a total of £7000 to take with her. When we gave her the money she thought we had won the lottery. She had never seen £7,000 let alone be handed the cash to do whatever she wanted. She bought herself a suitcase and we helped her to buy outfits for all of the relatives she would meet in India. She was like a little girl. I had never seen my mum giggle and yet she stood in stores, surrounded by expensive clothes, which she knew she could afford, and would giggle. We would stand together giggling at different cloth types. We would giggle together at the old Asian man who would be looking at us, smiling, and we teased our mother about him and his hunt for a fourth wife. She wants to spend some of the money to strengthen the walls around her parents' old house in India, which have been weakened over the years. She wants to help pay for the wedding of one of her nieces in India. She wants to spend some of the money on proper headstones for her parents' graves. We sat up past midnight on one occasion, eating cakes with her and her friends. We watched American chat show programme on which the lesbian guests were cheating on one another. Mum was aghast at what she was seeing and hugely confused about how these women could have children...or make children! We laughed a lot that night.

Today we are all at the airport with her. We have bought her a simple mobile phone and spent weeks teaching her how to use it. I watch her as she leaves for the gate with my older sisters, her grandchildren and I am thankful to whatever power is out there for giving her these days of joy and freedom. I watch her as she walks away and I know right there that my children will never face the struggles faced by my mum. They will never have to face the struggles faced by any of us siblings. Their lives will not be constrained by religion, culture or customs- I will do my upmost to make sure of it.

I love you mum, you are our silent warrior.

7 YASMIN

No one wants to talk about the sexual abuse that's present in the Asian community. People want to pretend it does not exist here. Maybe it's not pretending, maybe some people actually *believe* that it does not exist in this community, where everyone prays, gives to the poor and has a faith. They are blind. Sexual abuse happens in this community just like any other, the difference is the victims don't talk about it. They can't talk about it. *If* they talk about it, *if* they point the finger then they too will be held responsible. *They must have encouraged it, they shouldn't have been keeping a boyfriend, they should have kept their bodies covered.* Lots of my friends have been sexually abused and what's the one thing they all have in common? No one reported it. It becomes really complicated really quickly. Even when your intentions are to report it, you find yourself in a position where saying nothing becomes the most sensible route. So you decide to take the sensible path and get on with your life hoping, that god or the universe will make sure your abuser gets their comeuppance. But then even the sensible route becomes harder and harder because as the victim, you want justice. You want to know that the person who committed this horrific act upon you will be punished. So you find the strength and decide you *will* speak up. You *will* do it, and be brave and stand tall. But what happens to your desire for justice when that same person who abused you is related to you? What happens when he is your uncle? Your father's youngest brother who lives in India and has a large family of his own? What happens when that same uncle also has a son who is married to *your* sister and has four children with her? It becomes really complicated really quickly. You soon stop thinking about your own justice and start to think about your sister, your nieces and nephews- what would happen to them if I pushed forward with my accusation? What about my mother? Dad would punish her surely. What about my father? My aunties and uncles would pick a side and it would not be mine, it would be their brothers' side. What about my own siblings? Would they believe me at the risk of their marriages falling apart? Or would they remain silent, never taking any side? Through the utterings of a few words, I would lose all the family I ever knew and ever had. You might find the courage to still push ahead, maybe you have a new partner or husband who backs you and wants justice served as much as you do. It doesn't matter if *your* family turn your back on you because you have someone to turn to, someone who will take care of you. But then the authorities fail you. You have to go to India and report the crime because it took place there. If the crime took place in your home country during a family visit then the police need to work with the Indian authorities to catch the perpetrator and bring him to justice. It all costs too much money, it's not a priority. What are the chances of the police pushing forward a case that took place all those years ago? For which there is no evidence just the words of a child against a man? You are offered counselling by a sympathetic police officer, stumped at what to do or advise. You take up the offer. You find the courage to go to the counsellor and talk to them about past hurts but the counsellor has little idea about the cultural issues that affect you. The overwhelming majority of counsellors are white and have little idea of our culture, the constraints we face as women and the ideology we are born and raised in. They listen to you as you tell them you are scared of pushing forward with an allegation because the family will shun you. The counsellors react by labelling that very act of shunning as heinous and say things like 'If that is how they deal with their daughter then you are better off without them.' They say that I will be better off all alone for the rest of my life rather than being part of *that* family. But it's not true. I won't feel better off without them. In fact, I would miss them. I have moments of intense rage towards them all for treating me the way they did and then I have moments of unbelievable loneliness and sadness where I wish things could go back to how they used to be. I wasn't brave enough to go to the authorities and report what had happened. I supressed the memories so deep into myself that they started to spill out of the seams of my very being. I found I started to discover who I really was at the age of thirty and I want to share my story with you. I want to tell you what happened to make me start my own journey of self discovery.

India was a strange yet familiar experience for me. I went there at the ages of 7, 10 and 12 with my siblings and parents. I discovered a whole new family living in a tiny village. There were aunts, uncles, cousins, grandparents - all manner of extended family members who lived in India. It was my dad, who as the eldest, was chosen to leave and build a new, more successful life in England away from the desperate poverty. All the family scraped enough money together to pay for airfare and a few months rent. Ever since then, dad has been sending money back to his family to help them with their living costs. I never liked it when the media picked up on stories like this and complained that some immigrants didn't contribute anything to the economy, they just came to the UK, stole jobs from British people and now send all their money back home. I don't understand what dad could have done differently. He had a shitty factory job and used his meagre wages to pay his rent, to buy food, to pay his taxes and where he had some money remaining, he sent it to his family in India to help them survive each day. What did the media want him to do? Piss it up the wall? Spend it all on alcohol? Buy a new car? Designer clothes? One year, my grandmother became ill and dad had to send a lot of money to pay her medical bills after all,

India doesn't have an NHS system. Another year, my niece was getting married so dad sent money to help with the dowry and wedding costs associated with a girl. It was the least he could do. That is what he would always say. After all, if it wasn't for them, we would not be in the fortunate position we are currently in. We would not have been born British citizens nor would we live in a country with such great education facilities, excellent health care and protection for people. Dad never broke the law. He never manipulated the immigration laws to get someone into the country. My grandparents wanted to visit the UK and so one year, dad applied for a visitor's visa for them and they were able to spend 6 weeks with us in the UK. They were glad to go back to India as their visa neared expiry. They hated the weather, the cramped house and found the food bland. India was all they knew, the open huts and the brown earth, so very different to the grey weather and brick houses of England. Dad got on well with everyone, he had no issues with the British people and on the whole, they were accepting of dad and of us. Mum was a housewife and had a similar temperament to dads. She relished her role as the housekeeper and did everything and more to keep things in order. She raised us all to be well mannered, polite and quiet. We were miniature versions of her, doing our very best to keep everyone else happy.

I remember the first time I stepped foot off the aeroplane and into India- the heat was astonishing. It just seemed to square up to you and then hit you hard enough to make you gasp. Within minutes you were irritable, uncomfortable and hot. The crowds that had gathered at the airport were a rabble of people, all shouting and pulling you towards their taxi or trying to direct your attention to whatever they were selling. Brown faces, foreheads beaded with sweat, the smell of body odour and the heat all mingled together making me feel like I was suffocating. Our relatives found us in the crowd and lead us to waiting transport and safety. Through the windows I saw people throwing themselves at the car, banging against the car, mimicking the act of eating food whilst their eyes searching ours, implored us to give them money. There was one man who was sprawled across the front of the car begging for food. My uncle, laughing, asked him to move and when he refused, my uncle pushed him off. They were used to these scenes and found them laughable. I was saddened and confused. There were young girls about the same age as me with tattered clothing and earth in their hair. They were begging, gesturing to their mouths and pointing to their stomachs. Food. My parents had seen this all before and continued their conversations with their relatives as though they were sat chatting to friends in a pleasant café somewhere. My cousins were delighted to see us even though they had never met us before. They kept asking if I was ok and whether I would like a sweet or a drink or something else. Nothing was too much. Two of my three uncles had large families and all lived next door to one another in the village. My third and youngest uncle lived and worked in Delhi. He had 2 sons who did not live with him but instead, lived with my older uncles in the village. My third uncle's wife had left him and so he sent his boys to the village, to work with their uncles until he remarried and had a new wife who could take care of the boys. He didn't return to the village because he had a well-paid job in Delhi and was able to regularly send money back. We went to visit him in Delhi and spent 2 nights with him in his apartment, which was tiny. He had laid down straw mats and blankets everywhere to make up enough beds for us - there were 12 of us in total. Mum and dad got the main bed and my smaller sisters were in the same room as them. I was on the floor in his lounge and had my cousins dotted around me on the floor. My uncle was on the sofa just behind me. I don't remember much about that first night except none of us slept very well because of the heat, the humidity, the noise and the occasional scurrying of insects across the floor. Our tour of Delhi started the following day. My uncle looked similar to my dad- just a lot younger and boyish. He was quiet and didn't say much. He was very respectful towards mum and towards his older brothers. We went to the local bazaar where he was well known by the local storekeepers. They would constantly stop us and ask us to enter their store and have a look around. Some were even pushing us into their store and forcing bottles of coke into our hands. Mum and dad would shake their heads and say no before taking the drinks out of our confused hands and handing them back to the owners who would then shake *their* heads and say 'No no please, they are children from abroad, let them drink it' and push the bottles back into our hands. It was a good tactic they used because as children, we were hot and bothered and we loved coke. It was only a matter of time before one of us started to sip from the luminous straw popping out of the bottle neck and that was it. The deed had been done and now we all *had* to sit with the storeowner and allow them to showcase whatever they were selling in the hope that we would buy from them. It was like an unwritten rule - your children accepted the drinks and so now, the least you can do is sit and look at what is being offered. Cue the ever flowing rolls of fabric, every colour and texture you could imagine, some with huge intricate thread work, others with garish stones and sequins. I don't know how many times my parents said no to the items being showcased before they let us go. When we walked down the streets, I was always flanked by my cousins or uncles or parents on either side. I never understood back then why I had protection at either side. I didn't even notice it. It's only when I look back now that I understand what was really happening. They were protecting me from the men. The recent media attention surrounding the rape and sexual harassment happening in India is not a new phenomenon, it's always been there. The difference is that the western media are only reporting these matters now. My cousins were well aware that a female alone by herself, even a child, was at risk. I did draw a lot of attention from the locals – my skin was very fair and my hair very curly. I did not look like an Indian girl. Our skin, our clothes and the way we spoke told the locals that we were foreigners and foreigners always drew gazes. My eldest sister was 12 at the time and was getting a lot of attention, so much so that mum stopped to buy her a long veil which she wrapped around her head so only her eyes were visible. We ate freshly grilled kebabs whilst sitting in a local park, chatting amongst ourselves. My dad and his brothers were talking about their younger years and laughing. There were fireworks being let off somewhere close to us. We could see them shattering high in the sky and bursting into different colours.

It was about dawn when I was awoken by him I think. My *shalwaar* was down and his hand was searching in my knickers. He stopped still when he saw me awake and slowly withdrew his hand whilst moving backwards until he was back on his couch. He lay himself back down and closed his eyes.

The following morning we left to go back to the village and I remembered having an unpleasant dream. He kissed my cheek goodbye and told me to be a good girl for my mum.

When we visited him again I was 10 years old. He had a new wife, she was 16 years old and they had moved to a house in Delhi. We had beds this time and again I awoke when I felt something crushing my chest. I realised quickly he was on top of me and I could not move. He was masturbating whilst laying on top of me and ejaculated on my clothes. He wiped the semen off once he had finished but there remained a wet patch on my yellow *kameez* which hardened by the morning. This time when we left, he kissed my forehead and told me I would get into trouble if I told anyone.

The last time I visited, I was 12 years old. There were arguments at my uncle's houses. My dad was shouting and my two uncles were shouting and the women were crying. I later found out that this was when it had been decided by dad that his eldest daughter, my sister, would marry the son of his youngest brother. My uncle, the child molester, would become my sister's father in law. My other 2 uncles were not happy with his decision. They wanted one of their sons to be the chosen one but dad was adamant. He said that his younger brother was confused and his brain must not be working correctly. That was the only good enough reason he could think of that explained how a father could abandon his only sons, and allow them to be raised by their uncles in a distant village. I think dad was trying to help in his own sort of way. He saw the 2 boys with no future, living with relatives, without the love of parents, stigmatised because their mother abandoned them first followed by their father and felt he had to help in any way he could. My sister was happy with the arranged marriage and so it went ahead. The village was lit up with bright lights and the musicians banged on their drums, singing and laughing. The women preened and fussed and giggled and danced. I watched as henna was painted onto my sister's hands, wrists, arms, feet and legs during the henna ceremony. There were women holding trays lined with fresh flowers, lit candles and pots of henna. The women swayed and danced with the trays adding henna to my sisters hair first and then on the hair of the groom. People lined up to bless them both, walking up to the couple, scooping a small amount of henna out of a nearby bowl and applying it to the hair of the happy couple. They followed this up by dipping their finger into a bowl of oil and touching their foreheads whilst blessing them. The bride and groom to be, sat together stealing glances at one another when they thought no one was looking. I remember my mum spent most of the ceremonies crying and being consoled by other females who knew her pain. I was sent into one of the bedrooms to find some more henna powder to mix up. He followed me and shut the door. I stood awkwardly as his hands fumbled under my *kameez* first, searching for something to pinch. When they failed to find nothing other than the flat chest of a child, the hands moved down and into my *shalwar*. He touched, pushed, pinched and stroked to his hearts content and I stared hard at floor. He told me to remain quiet and to keep looking at the floor. Once content with touching me, he took both of my hands and placed them on his groin. I could feel his erect penis. He pulled down his *shalwaar* enough for his penis to be exposed and I stood there, in complete disgust, looking at this brown log, stood tall and ugly. He then instructed me to masturbate him, showing me calmly how to do it. I started to cry, ever so quietly but he closed his eyes. He stopped me suddenly and then turned me around pulling my *shalwar* down to my ankles. He then ejaculated on my buttocks. I don't remember much else of that night, how the night ended or what I ate. I do remember watching fireworks though towards the end of the night and laughing with my cousins every time they exploded with a loud bang, filling the skies with bright colours and smoke. A few weeks later, my now married sister stayed in India whilst the rest of us returned home and carried on with our lives.

The seasons came and went quickly and I grew into a woman. The high school experience happened quickly for me and I floated through those years with absolutely no interest in boys. I don't even remember a celebrity that I had a crush on. My sisters started to whisper to one another about me being a lesbian when I got to the age of 17. This was less to do with the fact that I had never had a boyfriend and more to do with my hatred towards men. On more than a few occasions, one of my sisters, a cousin, a friend and even a teacher sat me down to talk to me about where the hatred stemmed from. Was it my father? Did he hurt me? Was I a lesbian? At that time I had blocked out the incidents in India. They were wiped clean from my mind and didn't exist for me. And so, my hatred towards men and complete lack of interest in them made me unsure of who *I* really was. Maybe I really was a lesbian but my religious beliefs stopped me from wanting to believe this. I watched lesbian pornography at 18 years of age to see if that was what I wanted but couldn't stand to watch more than a few minutes- it did nothing for me but make me wince when they put their fingers inside one another. Physically, I felt myself tensing up and still, my mind would not give up the memories that were buried. By the time I was 19, my parents were pestering me about marriage. They worried when I said I never wanted to get married, they thought I was naïve and possibly mad. The opportunity came to visit India again for a holiday and I immediately said no. My family were shocked at my refusal of a free holiday but they respected my decision, assuming it was related to the amount of university work I had. I don't know why I refused to go, perhaps subconsciously I knew what was waiting for me. I remember the nausea that crept up and a feeling of impending doom overtaking my senses whenever India was mentioned. University was difficult and I found myself getting close to a boy and then hating him for no reason. It was such a violent swing of emotions. I could not wait to see him, talk to him, hear his laugh and yet once he was with me, I needed to be as far away as I could from him. He didn't seem to mind and constantly reassured me that it was ok. Slowly we got closer and closer. We started to hold hands and kiss one another. As the months went by, the kissing became more frequent, heavier and more passionate. One evening whilst we were kissing, he pressed up against me. And it was as if someone was playing a clip from an old film back to me. It was as if, I was transported back in time and I was there again. On the bed in a stuffy house, the air thick with humidity and the weight of someone on top of me, crushing my chest. I could even smell him, and hear his raspy breath in my ear. I pushed him off me screaming at him, calling him a dirty bastard and shouting for him to get out. I was hysterical. He tried to calm me down but I was utterly hysterical. I was gasping for air between my sobs and he sat there, with tears in his eyes watching me break apart. He eventually left me with my thoughts after I pleaded repeatedly with him to do so. As soon as he left, I packed up my things, posted a letter to him telling him I'm sorry but it's over, and went home. I enrolled to complete my degree at another university, 200 miles south. I pushed the flashback out of my mind and boxed up the memory of me sobbing hysterically. I found I was easily able to take a memory I disliked and box it away somewhere in mind. It was like filing away something in a vast library. I filed him away in my library along with the day of my first flashback. We exchanged e mails a few times but that soon fizzled out- I had lost all interest in him.

I found myself pulled towards humanitarian work and roles that involved helping others. Whilst at my second university, I secured a job helping immigrants to learn English, Maths and basic I.T. I also made a new group of friends, all from different backgrounds and different walks of life. We had the same interests and worked in broadly similar circles. We would often go out together as a group during the evenings and weekends. I met Alistair during one of our nights out. I found myself staring at him when he was looking elsewhere and then turning away when he did look my way. When he came over to talk to me I listened to him and answered all of his questions. We talked for hours about everything. We discussed politics and philosophy, immigration, culture and xenophobia – he was so intellectual. He challenged some of the views I held and I made him see some things from another perspective. By dawn I was so giddy from talking all night and so tired from the lack of sleep that I told him I really liked him but I would never be able to have a relationship with him because I tried that once and it didn't work. Just like that I said it. He thought I was telling a joke and laughed at first before realising I was telling him that this girl sat in front of him, at the age of 22, had never had a proper relationship. He asked me if I was scared of men and I said I thought so but was not sure. He held my hand and continued to talk to me about politics and religion and I was the happiest I had been for a long time. I told Alistair that my religion forbade me from having sex before marriage and he seemed to accept that. I didn't feel panicked when I kissed him and I would let him hold me and touch me. He had sparkling blue eyes framed with dark thick lashes and milky skin. I would spend hours running my hands through his thick dark curly hair and would pull his earlobes and poke his cheeks. I would kiss his mouth, nuzzle his neck and bury myself in his arms. He loved me. He adored me. We were together for 8 years before he told me he no longer loved me anymore. I had just turned 30.

In all honesty, things had started to become stale after 3 years. Alistair thought I would be ready to have a physical relationship with him once we were married but I told him that I was not ready for marriage and would not be for a number of years. The word marriage started to mean sex for both of us and when we talked about marriage, we were actually talking about sex. I just couldn't do it. I couldn't picture us doing *it*. The thought of it repulsed me and I would feel my body tensing up. The act repulsed me. The male penis repulsed me. The thought of someone putting something inside of *my* body repulsed me. Alistair tried on a number of occasions, we tried music, candles, a gentle approach and alcohol too but nothing worked. I would become hysterical sometimes and angry at other times. He coped well with me and my reactions, always remaining calm and never getting angry with me. I however, got angry with myself. There were parts of my mind within which I knew I had to delve but I did not have the strength. Coupled with this was the feeling of absolute fear of what I might find, how I would react and what the consequences could be. There were a few occasions where I would sit in silence, close my eyes and think back to India. I would see the brown earth, the man sprawled across the bonnet of the car, the small girl with muddy grey hair gesturing for food, grilled kebabs, fireworks, the faces of my cousins and then I would feel my breaths quickening, my chest tightening and I would open my eyes and familiarise myself with my surroundings. I would look around my room and focus on the bookcase, the table, the statues and the TV. Slowly, my breathing would soften and I would stand up and turn on the television. I could change what I was thinking about, file it away and concentrate on something else at the flick of a button in my mind.

Alistair and I carried on in our nonsexual relationship. We lived as best friends, who kissed, cuddled, talked and said I love you to each other every day. We introduced ourselves as a couple and did everything together. Alistair never stopped me chasing my dreams regardless of whether that meant a move to a different city or country. I always felt like I needed to move further and further away from my family. He had the opportunity of some work abroad for a few weeks and so left with my blessing.

I continued to keep in touch with mum and dad via the phone and occasionally emailed and text my siblings. I would visit the family home twice a year. I was racked with guilt for not visiting them often, they were old and troubled. They didn't have much money and the pressure to support family in India still remained. They argued a lot and my siblings were caught between the rows. During one visit when my mum was telling me about the latest fight she and dad had, I told her not to worry and that things would be ok. My older sister who was stood there said 'Wise words, I guess you can be full of wise words when you're never here.' I became defensive and asked her what she meant. 'You know exactly what I mean. You're never here are you? *We* are all here. *We* have to live with this shit day in and day out and you just gallivant from one city to another, from one country to another. You don't care about them. You come twice a year, sit around, give your meaningless advice and then fuck off again.' I remember telling her it was her choice to buy a house so close to mum and dad and she knew what she was getting into. I went further and said her choices in life were her own fault and she shouldn't blame me if I wanted a different life. At the time I was angry at her. Angry at her for speaking the truth out loud. Now, today, I am angry at my reaction. I understand her frustration, she doesn't want to begrudge me a life but she wants me to help. She is right, together we are a stronger force and we should all be there for our parents. I wish I had told her on that very day why I didn't like to come home. Why I was selfish and kept myself away. Why I was always running. But I didn't say anything like that at the time and our relationship continued to break down further. My phone calls to mum and dad continued but it became easier to ignore my siblings. Occasionally I would get a text message saying the obligatory 'I hope you are ok and things are going well for you' and I would respond with similar words. This way, we were not cutting ourselves off from one another completely and we had a route back into each other's lives.

Alistair told me he was no longer in love with me one afternoon after I asked him about a printed email I found in his bag. It was from an unknown female and spoke about how she thought about him often, even though she was in China. The email detailed the sights she had visited and the people she had encountered. It told of her excitement at journeying forth to Australia and the golden beaches stretched out in front of her. Initially the e mail confused me. I had never heard of Amelia Campbell, Alistair had never mentioned her. And yet, there was so much familiarity in the e mail. Like good friends writing to one another. As I continued to read and make sense of the letters and words I felt the blood rushing to my cheeks and I could hear my heart thudding in my ears. I read the email twice before finally settling on the last paragraph where she wrote

'I never got to properly thank you for dinner, breakfast, lunch, dinner and breakfast....I guess you tend to thank someone as you leave them or when the night ends but what can a girl do when all the events happen continuously? I was barely able to catch my breath to say the words...so here they are. THANK YOU. I hope we can shut ourselves away again when I return one day. I will e mail you.'

I have read about women and their reactions when they find the conclusive proof that their partners have been cheating. There is rage, anger and sadness. There is shouting, screaming, crying and begging. My initial reaction was numbness. I felt nothing at all. I took the email and went to his computer, pulled out his chair and sat down facing his desk. His desk was always messy. Alistair lived with me in my little flat whenever he was able to secure work close to me. We had decided to use the second bedroom as a study and so Alistair had one half of the room and I had the other. My side had piles of books, bean bags and a small side table which often held my mug of steaming, comforting tea. Alistair's side had an ugly metal desk that was inundated with papers, books, stationery and opened mail. His laptop sat in the middle of it all. I had never looked at his laptop before. In all the years we were together, I had never looked at his computer or his phone. There was just never any need to. I had my own computer and quite often, we would sit in the study together whilst he would tap away on his keypad and I would leaf through a book taking mouthfuls of chai. Occasionally, I would repeat something I had just read to get his reaction and we would start a debate. And here I was now, sitting at his desk, opening the cover of his laptop. The machine sprung to life, there was no passwords to input or folders to find. A notification popped up telling me there was new mail. One click took me to his inbox and there I started to trawl through his emails. There was nothing suspect on the first 4 pages and I nearly stopped looking until I felt a strong urge to check his junk mail, his trash folder and his drafts folder. It was in his drafts folder where I found some more emails- all from different women. Natalie, Sara, Zlatka, Imogen. In his junk folder I found more emails from different women: Katie, Lyndsey, Hazel, Charlotte, Danielle. I read every email I found. Some were explicit, thanking him for a great night and detailing all the things they would do if he would meet with them again. Others were angling for a relationship and sending him further emails demanding to know why they were being ignored. I started to look through his sent folder and found numerous e mails back. Some to women giving them a date, time and place and other emails to women telling them he had made a mistake sleeping with them and his head was all over the place. He wrote that he was with a loving, gentle and beautiful woman whom he loved very much and he had just made a mistake. I had about 3 hours before he would return so I walked over to my book pile and found my diary. I started to go through my diary, which detailed every occasion when Alistair was away, and matched it up to the emails. The picture coming to life was that whenever Alistair was going away for weeks a time with work, he either finding a new woman to sleep with or arranging to meet women he had already slept with. Imogen seemed to be a favourite of his. I read each and every word they exchanged, torturing myself. Alistair was writing things like 'I can't wait to be inside of you again', 'I can't wait to hear you come', ' I can't get your taste out of my mouth'. And Imogen was responding with 'My body is all yours, do what you want with it, just make me come like you did last time', 'This time, I'm going to fuck you until YOU get sore.'

The mind is a wonderfully complex organ. It hides memories away that are too painful for the owner to deal with and then releases them, in the form of flashbacks for the person to slowly come to terms with. I read all the words but my mind did not process them. It's like when you read a book, you find yourself thinking about the scene that is being described. You imagine the face of the hero and the villain as you read about them. Sometimes you can see and even smell the meadow and the wildflowers being described, the birds singing in the sunshine. I imagined nothing when I read Alistair's emails. I pictured nothing in my mind and like a machine, I just processed the words making sense of what had really been happening in Alistair's life over the past few years. Once or twice I had sudden flashes, images in my mind of a naked Alistair and a naked white blonde gasping but I pushed them out. I thought about how many things he had in my flat and whether we had a case large enough for him to take everything with him today. I found a medium sized case and some overnight bags which I lay near his desk. I made myself a cup of tea and sat on my bean bag, waiting to hear his key in the door.

When he arrived he started to say something but his words trailed away when he saw the empty case and his open laptop. He stepped towards it and I watched his face change when he saw the email from Amelia I had left on his desk. He pressed a key on his laptop bringing the machine to life and was greeted by rows of all the emails he had sent. He sat at his desk and put his head in his hands taking deep breaths. He sobbed whilst telling me he was sorry and that he loved me but he was not in love with me and had not been for a very long time. He told me he had never wanted to hurt me, he had only wanted to protect me. He apologised countless times and sobbed like a little lost boy. I asked him if it was the sex, did he see these other women because I could not have penetrative sex with him? He said he wasn't sure why he did what he did but said he was in a very bad place. I asked him whether we could be together if I slept with him but he continued to sob and apologise and say no. He was no longer in love with me. When he eventually left with all of his things, I started to clean the flat - there was dust everywhere. When I had finished I put on my coat and walked out into the rain and to the local supermarket, open 24 hours a day. I bought some tampons and some vodka and made my way home in the dark. I mixed the vodka with coke and started taking gulps of the drink. My drinking was rhythmic, glass up, take a gulp, squeeze my eyes shut, swallow, breathe and glass down. It took about 10 minutes before I started to feel a little drunk and so I carried on, pouring myself another tumbler full of coke and vodka before sitting back down and starting again. When I started to giggle to myself, having nearly fallen down, I stumbled my way into the bathroom with a tampon. It was there that I tried to penetrate myself. At first, I couldn't get the tampon any further than a centimetre but more alcohol made me less tense. I found myself thinking about all the things I had to do and all the adventures I could go on now that I was single, in an attempt to make me forget that I was trying to insert a tampon. When I started to bleed from pushing and pushing, I stopped, took the tampon out, saw the tip was bloody and I broke down right there in my bathroom. The anger came like a giant wave and knocked the breath out of me. How could he do this to me? I didn't deserve this, why did he do it? It must have been because I can't have sex with him. I am pathetic. I am 30 and I am pathetic. What the hell is wrong with me? Then the wave of panic hit me. I was now 30 and had nobody and no future with anybody. It looked as though getting a partner was going to be impossible. I am all alone now. There will be no one coming home to me or kissing my forehead. There will not be anyone in my bed. All his food was still in the kitchen, I had to let him know. I called him and told him that he needed to come and get his food. He said he didn't want it. I started to cry, I wailed at him through the phone. He was crying too. I begged him to come back. I promised him I would find a way to make him love me again, I promised I would have sex with him, I begged him again and again. And he just sobbed and told me he was no longer in love with me and that he was sorry. He didn't love me anymore. I spent the next few hours drifting in and out of consciousness, dreaming about India and monsters and Alistair's blue eyes to then awake and remember that something terrible had happened. And the wall of grief would hit me and the tears would start all over again.

The loneliness I felt for the next few months was something I had never experienced before. It was not just the absence of Alistair that made me feel so alone but also the absence of talking to someone about the ordeal. My family were not even aware I was with someone let alone that he was white and not a Hindu so I could not go to them. My sisters would not have approved and although they would have lent a sympathetic ear, it would have been false. My friends who knew of Alistair did not know of my past and were of the opinion that he was a deplorable person for cheating on me with numerous women and then leaving me. I did not wholly agree with their conclusions but could not tell them about the real relationship that Alistair and I had shared for the last 8 years. I realised just how alone I really was. Here I was, a British Hindu female, born and bred here in England with English and Indian values and yet, I had no idea who I really was. When I introduced myself as British I would be asked, where are you really from? Only once the enquirer heard that my parents were from India were they satisfied and would stop asking more questions. So I did not feel British, and when I had visited India, I was treated like a foreigner so I didn't feel Indian either. I tried writing things down but I was never any good at that. The weeks turned colder and the nights came quicker. Alistair was never far from my thoughts. During the first few weeks, I would walk around the flat and have conversations with him pretending he was sat at his desk tapping away. I would read something astonishing whilst sat on my bean bag and talk to him about it. I think I was mentally unravelling. I started to look for teaching opportunities abroad and was offered a role in South Africa teaching English with decent, tax free pay and accommodation. I was offered the role on a Wednesday afternoon as I walked back to my flat through the wind and the rain. I very nearly did not answer the call as the caller ID flashed up as anonymous. Shelton, the learning manager, told me the start date was in 2 months' time and they would now start the process of getting references and then liaising with me so I could obtain my working visa and complete a number of other administrative tasks. I noticed the sign for the very first time that day even though I walked past *that* store nearly every single day. Richard Shannon-Renowned psychotherapist specialising in couples counselling and sex therapy. I can't remember what exactly it was that drew my eye to the sign in the window but I found myself taking a picture and then hurrying back to my flat. I left a message for Richard that very evening.

A week later I was sat in warm room. The walls were a rich cream and there were 2 large floor lamps. They had the same dark wood holding them up and a large cream lampshade. The room was bathed in a warm light and instantly I felt reassured. The coffee table, the side table and the small table in the corner were all made of the same dark chocolate coloured wood as the lamp. The large cream fabric sofa looked inviting but I chose the smaller lounging chair next to the sofa. The sofa just seemed too big for me and I wasn't sure whether I was supposed to lie down, sit to the right, sit to the left or sit in the centre. The chair I chose was more like those sun loungers you find on a beach. All my body fitted on the perfect length and it was extremely comfortable. I never understood how Richard managed to keep the room smelling like it did. It always smelt of new carpets and new furniture but I couldn't understand how this was possible when he had been using it for years. I never did ask him about that and it bothered me greatly. Richard shook my hand when I first entered the room and I didn't look at him, I looked at his brown shiny shoes. Only once I was on my chair did I look at him. He had his head down and was filling in some forms, scribbling something on paper resting on his dark brown little desk. He had brown hair which looked like it hadn't been styled, it just sort of fell about his face. He wore glasses and had a nicer face than I expected. He was carrying a bit of weight around his middle but you could only see that if you really looked. He had good thighs-Alistair would have hated him. He hated anyone with good sized thighs as he would say. Alistair was born with a thin frame and although I always found this appealing, he wanted to gain weight. He would succeed around his middle, his arms and even his face but his thighs always remained slim. Richard had plumper thighs. Eventually I decided that Richard had a kind face, a sort of face that invited you to talk. The first meeting consisted of me retelling my story to Richard without shedding a single tear. I told him how Alistair and I had met, how much I loved him and how he had betrayed me. I told him about the nights of crying and about trying to insert a tampon to try and make me ok. I told him about my job offer in South Africa and how I had decided to try and fix myself before I left by booking in with him. He listened and nodded along, smiling at the right times and showing sympathy at other times. He asked me about my current job, my daily routine, my ex partners, my family and my friends. He took interest when I told him I don't talk to my family much and asked further questions around this. When I told him about my confrontation with my sister and how hurt I was having heard what she really thought of me, he said he found my anger towards my sister odd. Richard said he understood my sister's frustrations but did not agree with her method of confrontation. He asked me why I did not visit them all more often and I replied telling him it was too far, the train tickets were too expensive, whenever I did call them all I would hear about would be the fights and finally because deep down none of them approved of the life I was living. He listened and nodded. When the session was drawing to an end he told me he could help me but it would be difficult. He said that he sensed there were areas that I had not spoken about, perhaps something in my childhood or a traumatic event. He said I needed to go home and think about my intentions and the real reason I decided to seek out his help now, with only months to go before I left for a new country. I found this quite funny and tried to explain to him that I decided to meet with him on a whim. It was just chance and nothing more. But he explained that he felt I had been running all of my life. He asked me to be honest with myself. He made me think about why I was away from my family? He made me think about my move away from university. Every time I encountered something difficult, every time something which could have been fixed went wrong, I ran away. I was laughing at his suggestions but deep down, something was niggling at me, making me feel nauseous.

On our second meeting, I went in to tell him I would not be seeing him again but instead, I told him of my memories of India. And then I broke. I was his last appointment and was with him for nearly three hours that evening. I had moments of silence, moments of sobbing and moments of talking. I told him about what I remembered. Over the next few weeks, he worked with me to help me to remember what had happened and helped me to start working through the old hurts.

It's really lonely where I am at the moment. I look forward to my sessions with

Richard on a weekly basis and I am making some really good progress. I often find that after leaving his sessions, I am exhausted and need to sleep. I knew I had issues but I never wanted to face them before, I never wanted to think about them. I sort of hoped that if I kept them buried then they would eventually disappear. But the mind is fascinating. I developed these little quirks in my personality instead. I couldn't let men be intimate with me but I convinced myself and others that it was because I was a bit quirky, funny, frigid and scared. I never took anyone of those words and investigated what they actually meant for me. What was I scared of? Why was I frigid?

I recently joined a dating site and have been on a few dates with men. I wonder if I will ever be in a position to have a normal relationship with someone one day and whether I will even have a family of my own. I rejected the job offer from South Africa in the end. Deep down, I knew that if I took the position, my therapy would stop. And although it was tempting to run away again, I found the courage to stay put and carry on seeing Richard. We have become close. He is fond of me and sometimes, I feel we are more than just therapist and patient. Sometimes, I feel like he is talking to one of his daughters. I have watched his kind eyes twinkle with tears when I have struggled with recalling those memories in India. I saw the same wetness in his eyes when he listened to me talk about feeling lonely and not wanting to go back to my lonely flat and tin of soup. I did visit home though. I didn't even tell them and turned up at mum and dads doorstep with a small case. They were elated to see me. Once the hugging and kissing was done, we sat and talked about everything that had been happening in the community, in the family and in India. I watched my parents as they filled me in on everyone else's business and knew right then that they had no idea of the things that had happened to me in India. I could never tell them either. I was too scared of their reaction. I was too scared of causing them pain. And I knew the consequences it would have on my sister. I made a decision then to continue as I was. To continue telling them I wasn't ready for marriage, to continue telling them I was not a lesbian, to continue telling them I didn't have a boyfriend and to continue fighting until they learnt how to accept me as I am.

I still see Richard. I hope we continue in this relationship and I hope I am fixed one day. I have already seen changes in my demeanour. I have already started to find some closure for everything that happened in India. Sometimes when you cannot get the justice you feel is owed to you, it is healthier to find your own closure. He took so much away from me; I will not allow him to take any more. I take each day as it arrives and look forward to whatever life has in store for me.

8 LETTER TO MY SISTER

I often sit and think about you. You pop into my mind when I least expect it and I always smile. Sometimes, the oddest thing I see makes me think about you. I often wonder what colour your hair is and how you wear it. Do you still wear it down and let it fly everywhere? Or do you tie it up and look professional? Are you still thin and tall? Do you still laugh a lot? Is your laugh still as loud as it used to be? Do you still cry at sad movies? Or when you see old people struggling in the street? I know this letter will never reach you but I had to write it. It's to help me deal with everything that happened.

I miss you. Mum misses you. She is old now and sometimes, I hear her crying in the middle of the night. She wears these huge glasses and looks comical to most people who see her but she likes them. Her eyes show the deep wrinkles that only come with a life of sorrow. Do you remember how grandma used to say that about mum's eyes? Eyes that have seen too much sorrow. Dad is old too. His hair has thinned and his beard is grey and white. He feels the cold most days and sits by the fire which blazes, even during the summer months. Sometimes I look at him and convince myself that he is not the same person I remember him to be, all those years ago. My heart does not want to accept the way he was all those years ago but my mind reminds me and I find myself pitying him. I watch him with one of my daughters, bouncing her on his lap, laughing as she coos and gurgles, taking delight in her reactions as he blows raspberry's on her belly. Mum sits beside him, waiting to take over, laughing with him at the sight of my daughter gurgling and smiling at them with her bright eyes. I watch them most days as they give their everything to this little girl and I feel an overwhelming sadness for them.

I still replay so many scenes in my head. As though they only took place yesterday. They always end differently in my head than they did in real life. Like the first time you said you did not want to get married. I tried to convince you that it was for the best. Do you remember that conversation? I said that he was a good match for you. I even said that I was a bit jealous that you were given to him. Secretly, I think I always liked him, I think I had a bit of a crush on him but I was 8 years old and stupid. I liked him because every time I saw him, he would give me a lollipop or some other sugary treat. I remember you just stared at me and didn't say anything for what seemed like an eternity. And then you said you didn't love him, you said you were seventeen and wanted to go to college and then university. I remember feeling happy when I told you that you could still go to those places, I thought you would be happy to know that dad wanted you to continue your education. He always said you were the cleverest one out of the family and that you would make something of yourself one day, you would make everyone proud. When I replay that conversation now, it always ends with me telling you to pack your things and the both of us running away from that village in Pakistan together. It never ends with the truth, it never ends with me skipping off excited at the prospect of new dresses and a sisters wedding to look forward to.

I remember when you refused to go shopping with mum and your in -laws to choose your wedding gold. Mum couldn't take it anymore, your constant refusals to accept that you were going to get married. She started to hit you. I have never seen something so sad in all of my life. You just sat on the floor, cowering, whilst mum hit you with both her fists, sobbing as she did it. I threw myself on top of you and shouted at mum to stop it, to stop being horrible. Dad's sisters dragged mum away from you and she carried on crying, sobbing on the floor, away from you. She told you it wasn't *her* decision, it wasn't *her* who made the decisions, it was dad. Dad said you had to get married and that was it. There was no discussion, his word was the law and you *had* to get married. You watched mum sitting on the hard floor, sobbing. You listened to her pleas to go through with this wedding for her sake. The honour of the entire family was with you. If you didn't go through with this then dad would continue to beat her. He would blame her and she would never hear the end of it. You sat on the floor listening. I remember being stood in the doorway crying. I hated watching you get beaten up but this time, my tears were also streaming because some of the fists landed on me when I tried to cover you. I watched as you got up, straightened your clothes, neatened your hair and said to mum ok, lets go and walked out of the house and into the waiting car. Your in-laws to be, who had been waiting in the car the whole time, looked at your swollen eyes, swollen face and asked if you had a headache. They saw the blood on your forehead and the tears you were wiping away. You said yes, you did have a headache. I asked you if you were ok once we had reached the goldsmiths and you said you were fine. You picked the gold jewellery that looked like leaves. It was the second most expensive set in the whole shop and your in laws looked a bit pale. But they still bought it for you. I smile when I think of that moment because I knew you were being mischievous. That was you giving them two fingers and saying 'right, if this is how it's going to be then I might as well make you squirm'. That was you saying, 'if I am the plane ticket for your son to make it to the shores of England then you *will* pay the top price'. You picked the most expensive fabrics and when your mother in law said it was too much money you said you wouldn't marry his son then. That was enough to make them pull out their rupees. I still remember that wink and smile you gave me when no one else was looking.

Dad was due any day and we all knew that meant your wedding day was close. I could see you were planning to do something. I remember hiding under the bed in the big room with the locked wardrobe, watching you creep in and trying to pick the lock to get your passport. I watched as you looked at the hinges, as you tried to look at the back of the wardrobe and as you rocked it to see how heavy it was. You couldn't do anything. You stood there for what seemed a long time and then walked out. I was in that room eating the sweets I had stolen from the kitchen. I still live off sweets and chocolate today, it is a habit I never grew out of.

Dad arrived with the rest of our sisters on a Wednesday afternoon. He hugged you for a long time and you started to cry. He wiped your tears and told you to stop being silly, you were a woman now. Saira and Zara were 3 and 4 then, I don't think they remember anything. You started shouting at dad, and raising your voice. You said you knew now this was all his doing, he had lied to you. This was supposed to be a holiday and he had lied to you. He hit you right across your face and told you to know your place. You said you would run away and he told you this was Pakistan, it wasn't England. He told you he would break your legs and make sure you never walked again. Mum stood in the corner silently crying. I remember your face then. Your beautiful eyes searched dads face for a long time and you asked him to reconsider. He hit you again. This time you walked to your bedroom and shut the door.

I remember the next day was your engagement ceremony. The boy would come with a ring and place it on your finger and you would be engaged. Two days after there would be a huge wedding. You looked so pretty dressed in the purple *shalwaar kameez*, the veil covering your forehead. He came and placed the ring on your slender finger and you didn't even look up. People threw rupees over you as you sat there, staring at your lap, at your now decorated finger. Your groom had garlands of money placed around his neck and he was laughing and joking with his family, his sisters, his brothers and his friends. Mum sat quietly next to you holding your hand and making small talk with the people stood around. Dad stood in the doorway laughing with your groom whilst placing a large golden turban on his head.

I remember the outfit you wore for your henna night. The moss green coloured, silk *shalwaar kameez*. You left your hair down and sat whilst we all danced around you, adding henna to your hands and to your feet. I even remember you

151

smiling at the children who were dancing like never before. I remember you staring hard at the floor whenever mum, dad or any of us approached you. I remember your hair being tied up by a women and pinned with yellow and gold flowers. I had never seen you so quiet before and I started to worry. I asked you if you were sure you were ok. I thought maybe I had done something wrong. You took me into your arms and sat me in your lap, resting your chin on my head. I felt so happy at that moment. I could smell your sweet perfume and feel the heat coming off you. I didn't move until dad lifted me up and away from you making me cry until you blew me a kiss and put your finger to your lips. I instantly quietened down and smiled back at you. I always wanted to see you happy. I would have done anything to see you happy.

The day before your wedding, mum and dad told me I was to be engaged. I didn't really understand what that meant but they told me I would have to wear a ring when I went back to England and once I had finished secondary school, I would come back and get married. I remember how upset you were for me. Dad hit you again for reminding him I was only 8 years old and that they were monsters for doing this. I remember you screaming at him, telling him he would burn in hell for dividing his daughters out to his relatives as though they were chunks of meat. I didn't understand why you were so upset, I was quite happy to have someone make a fuss of me, give me a new dress to wear and then have this beautiful gold ring with pink stones placed on the fourth finger of my right hand. I got scared when I saw the man I was supposed to marry. He had a big moustache and looked the same age as dad. I remember crying at night after the ceremony finished and you comforting me. I remember what you said to me that night too, you promised me that you would never let it happen to me. You said you would make sure mum and dad changed their minds about forcing us to marry. I never knew what you meant but I suddenly felt safe.

The night before your wedding, I remember how strong the smell was from all the curries being prepared cooked for your big day. The men we had hired cooked all night in these huge pots. They looked like giant sized cauldrons, sitting on top of flames, bubbling away tenderising the meat and the lentils. The *tandoor* was glowing orange in the corner of the yard roasting the dozens of chickens left in there and dough was prepared by the maids ready to make naan breads the following day. You sat quietly on your bed whilst everyone danced around you. I wonder if you ever took notice of mum who didn't join in. She just watched you from the corner of the room and occasionally dabbed at her eyes. I always wonder what was going through her mind at that very moment. We never talk about that night.

A few weeks ago we watched a Bollywood film. I always think of you when this happens because I remember how much you hated them. We stumbled across this film when we were all sat flicking through the many Asian TV channels that mum subscribes to now. I was there with mum, dad and all three of my little ones. We decided to watch the film because dad liked the actress in the movie and had heard one of the songs. You must be surprised to be reading this- dad watching films? Listening to songs? Knowing who these Bollywood heroines are? He has mellowed a lot my wonderful, beautiful sister. He watches films now and enjoys some of the songs too. The film was about family. There was this large happy Indian family, they had wealth, success, power and were generally good people. The father was really arrogant though and although he loved his children, he had very high and unrealistic expectations of them. One of his children decided she did not want to marry the boy dad had picked out for her, she wanted to marry of her own choosing. And her own choice was this other boy who was lovely but really poor. In the film, both the boys are really nice. The rich one understands that the girl he is arranged to be married to is in love with another and tries to do the right thing and not marry her. I liked him. I wish she had married him. The poor boy that the girl loved was also lovely and would make her laugh a lot. He was always playing practical jokes but had no job, little education and was of low caste. The girl knew her father would never move on his decision and she would *have* to marry the rich guy. She killed herself. She couldn't shame her father by running away with someone that she loved, she couldn't marry someone she didn't love and she didn't want to marry someone because it had been arranged. She said it would destroy three lives, hers, her husbands and the boy she actually loved. She was so stuck between her love of her parents and her love of this boy that it seemed easier for her to commit suicide and take herself out of the equation instead of hurting the people she loved. The film then concentrated on the aftermath and how the father went into isolation. He banned music and any forms of art from his life- anything that reminded him of what she did. He never grieved for her. The mother would sob quietly and alone but the father never shed a tear. The boy she wanted to marry-Ajay- ended up getting a job working for the dad and the story focused on the dad and Ajay's relationship. Ajay knew that the old man he worked for was the father of the love of his life but the father had no idea that Ajay was the man his daughter left this world for. Ajay would talk to someone imaginary all the time and when the old man questioned him about this he would tell him that the love of his life was always with him. She would talk to him, they would sing together and laugh together. Years passed and the old man's youngest daughter started to like someone else too. The dad became angry and said he would gladly lose another daughter before suffering

153

the humiliation of seeing a living daughter marry a low caste boy. Ajay intervenes when the girl is about to run away and it all climaxes when Ajay shows the dad a letter that his first daughter had left. The letter said she felt she had no other choice but to take her own life so that her father's heart might soften towards those in love. See, she sacrificed her own life so that her father would change for her brothers and sisters. The father broke down when he read the letter and asked Ajay if she was in the room with them and he said yes, she was always here because she lived on in their hearts. The father let his daughter marry the boy and even danced at their wedding.

This film broke dad.

At first we thought he was having heart trouble because he was shaking but then we heard the wails. He was sobbing. I have never heard him or seen him in such a state. Mum rushed to him and tried to comfort him. I rushed up and tried to hug him but he carried on sobbing. He said he had made many mistakes, mistakes too big to forgive. He said 'What have I done? Look what I did.' He asked mum for forgiveness, he said 'I ripped your child from you, please forgive me. I ripped our child from us. I killed her. It is all on me.'

That's when I knew he always blamed himself for the day you killed yourself. Even though he would tell everyone that you were wrong to take your life. Even though he would say that you had committed a sin and we should all pray for your soul. He misses you like we all do. They all cried. You know, I'll never forget the scene that morning, the look on mums face when she opened your bedroom door. I was stood there too, in shock, unable to cry. Mum fell to the floor, screaming. Others rushed to the door, their mouths open and their eyes wide. Dad was suddenly pushing past me and mum saw him. She became hysterical and started to hit dad. Dad just stood there in disbelief looking at your face and the blood soaked sheets. He had a massive heart attack and we had to take him to the hospital where he stayed for the next week. Mum stopped talking for the next 2 days.

When grandma came to the house after news got out, she started to hit mum. She hit her own daughter and mum just sat there and let her. She said to mum 'I told you not to do this, didn't I tell you not to do this?' Grandma wouldn't grieve with everyone else, she just stayed in your room for days, crying and holding your picture. Eventually she let mum sit with her, on your bed, and they would cry together, mum sobbing in grandma's lap.

Your funeral was so strange. The entire village had been buzzing just a week or so earlier, preparing for your wedding. I noticed the wedding bunting still up around the village as they prayed and lowered your body into the ground. Dads face didn't move at all. He just stared into nothingness. His face was a pale grey colour. Mum cried quietly into her shawl and stood far away from Dad. Aunty Saira cried a lot for you, you two were quite close weren't you? Grandma had to walk away. His family were crying too. I don't know what they were more upset about, their son's future being dashed or you leaving this earth.

You kept your promise though. We came back to England and mum and dad just changed. They started to sleep in the same room and we were allowed to go into town with our friends. I didn't have to wear my headscarf anymore. We started to get spending money and dad let us out with friends. I eventually married of my own choosing. You kept your promise. Mum and dad never spoke about you. They had you buried in Pakistan next to grandad, mum knew you would have liked that. Mum prays for you every Friday. I hear her crying quietly sometimes. There are pictures of you everywhere. My favourite one of you was when you went to Alton Towers on a school trip and your friend Nita took a picture of you whilst you were day dreaming on the coach. Mum keeps that picture of you on her bedside cabinet. Dad made a collage of all the pictures he had of you- from being a baby to just before we left for Pakistan. He has that on the wall of their bedroom.

Mum and dad are closer now. Things here are much better. Sometimes, they still fight over small things but it's nothing like it used to be. Dad started going to the mosque more often to pray. Mum stopped going out with her friends and to community gatherings. She stays at home a lot now. They gave all of us freedom once you sacrificed yourself. Losing their daughter was too painful. They realised that they would rather have a daughter who doesn't keep their family honour and marries of her own choice instead of not have a daughter at all. Dad kept the letter you wrote. I know he has read it out for mum a few times. I know he keeps it in his suitcase which he hides under his bed. Sometimes I hear him crying in the bedroom. When he stops, I hear the soft clicks of his suitcase clasps shutting and I know then that he has been reading your letter. I think it makes him feel better, to read your words that tell him he wasn't to blame, that you hope no one will blame themselves or be angry at you.

Sometimes I wish you had gone through with the marriage, the rapes, the abuse- whatever you needed to endure to get back to England. You could have divorced him then. At least I would still have you in my life. But then I remember how brutal life was back then. And I know, deep in my heart, that things would never have changed the way they did for us when you died. I pray for you. Not because I think you committed a sin by taking your life, but because I miss you. I cry when I think of you sitting there knowing you were going to end your life. I cry for you when I think of how scared you must have been when you saw your blood pour out. I cry when I remember how you were laid on the bed, in your wedding outfit and all your gold, stained with dark red. I read that when you lose a lot of blood, it's like falling asleep. I pray it was like that for you. I pray it was a sharp, few moments of pain and then you went to sleep. I pray it was like that for you. Your skin was cold against mine when I tried to wake you up. I cry when I think of these things. I miss you terribly. We named our first daughter after you- she is definitely mum and dad's favourite. At first they couldn't even say her name without thinking about you and crying but now they bounce her on their laps, kiss her, cuddle her, spoil her and are so over protective. She is their second chance. She has eyes just like you and has the same quiet temperament you had. Our little Sabrina. She would have been your favourite too.

I know this letter will never reach you but I had to write it. It's to help me deal with everything that happened. It's to make sure your memory lives on way past any of us. Sleep well my beautiful sister.

End.

Printed in Great Britain
by Amazon.co.uk, Ltd.,
Marston Gate.